Contents

TRUEBOND PUBLISHING

What Women Really Want From A Man

Understanding Love Through Her Eyes

This book was professionally typeset on Reedsy.
Find out more at reedsy.com

III   Respect and Partnership

V   The Long Game

Introduction

The Great Mystery (That Isn't Actually That Mysterious)

Let's start with some uncomfortable truth-telling, shall we?

If you've picked up this book, chances are you've found yourself scratching your head at least once (or a hundred times) wondering what the hell women actually want. Maybe you've had relationships that started strong but fizzled out for reasons you couldn't quite grasp. Perhaps you've heard "you just don't get it" more often than you'd like to admit. Or maybe you're simply tired of feeling like you're playing a game where everyone else knows the rules except you.

Here's the thing: you're not alone, and you're not stupid. But you might be looking in the wrong places for answers.

The Great Lie We've All Been Sold

For decades, men have been fed a steady diet of contradictory advice about what women want. Movies tell us it's grand romantic gestures. Magazines suggest it's six-pack abs and expensive cars. Your buddy at work swears it's about being an "alpha male" who doesn't show emotion. Meanwhile, your sister insists women want sensitive guys who cry during commercials.

No wonder you're confused.

The truth is, most of the conventional wisdom about what women want is either outdated, oversimplified, or just plain wrong. It's based on stereotypes, marketing tactics, and the kind of surface-level thinking that treats women like a different species rather than, you know, actual human beings with individual thoughts, feelings, and desires.

Why This Book Exists

This book exists because the conversation about what women want has been dominated by extremes. On one side, you have the pickup artist crowd treating relationships like a conquest game. On the other, you have well-meaning but vague advice about "just being yourself" that doesn't actually tell you how to be a better version of yourself.

What's been missing is the middle ground: practical, research-backed insights that treat both men and women as complex individuals while acknowledging that there are some patterns worth understanding.

I wrote this book after talking to hundreds of women across different ages, backgrounds, and relationship stages. I interviewed relationship therapists, read academic studies, and yes, I made plenty of my own mistakes along the way. What emerged wasn't a magic formula or a secret code, but rather a clearer picture of what healthy, lasting relationships actually look like.

What Makes This Different

This isn't another book that will teach you pickup lines or manipulation tactics. It won't promise that following seven simple steps will guarantee romantic success. And it definitely won't treat women like puzzles to be solved rather than people to be understood.

Instead, this book will help you:

Understand the fundamentals that actually matter in relationships, not the superficial stuff that gets all the attention.

Develop genuine skills like emotional intelligence, communication, and partnership that will serve you in every relationship, not just romantic ones.

See patterns without stereotyping, recognizing common desires and needs while respecting individual differences.

Build authentic confidence that comes from being a genuinely good partner, not from pretending to be someone you're not.

Create lasting connections based on mutual respect, understanding, and genuine compatibility.

The Reality Check You Need

Before we dive in, let's get one thing straight: there is no universal answer to what all women want, just like there's no universal answer to what all men want. Women are individuals with their own preferences, experiences, and non-negotiables. Anyone who tells you otherwise is selling you something.

However, there are some fundamental human needs that most people share, regardless of gender: feeling respected, understood, valued, and genuinely cared for. There are communication styles that tend to work better than others. There are relationship dynamics that research shows lead to greater satisfaction and longevity.

This book focuses on those patterns while always remembering that the woman in front of you is a unique individual, not a representative of her entire gender.

How to Use This Book

This book is designed to be read straight through, as each chapter builds on the previous ones. But life is messy, and sometimes you need help with a specific situation right now. Each chapter is also designed to stand alone if you need to jump to a particular topic.

You'll notice that every chapter includes:

Real-world examples (with details changed to protect privacy) that illustrate the concepts in action.

Practical exercises that help you develop new skills and awareness.

Action steps you can implement immediately.

Common pitfalls to avoid, because knowing what not to do is often as important as knowing what to do.

At the end of each chapter, there's a "Key Takeaways" section that summarizes the main points. Use these for quick reviews or when you need a refresher.

A Word About Vulnerability

Here's something that might make you uncomfortable: becoming a better partner requires becoming more vulnerable. Not in a weak, needy way, but in an authentic, emotionally available way. This might go against everything you've been taught about masculinity, but the research is clear: emotional intelligence and the ability to form genuine connections are among the most attractive qualities a person can have.

This book will challenge some of your assumptions about what it means to be a strong man in a relationship. If you're open to that challenge, you're going to discover that real strength includes emotional awareness, that confidence includes the ability to admit when you're wrong, and that leadership in a relationship looks a lot more like partnership than dominance.

What You Can Expect

If you commit to the principles in this book, here's what you can realistically expect:

You'll have better conversations with the women in your life, romantic or otherwise. You'll find yourself getting into fewer pointless arguments and resolving conflicts more effectively when they do arise. You'll develop the kind of emotional intelligence that makes you a better friend, colleague, and partner.

Most importantly, you'll stop feeling like you're constantly guessing what women want and start building the kind of genuine connections that make the question irrelevant.

One Last Thing

The title of this book might suggest it's about changing yourself to please women. That's not what this is about at all. This is about becoming the kind of person who can build authentic, lasting relationships with anyone. The principles you'll learn here will make you a better partner, but they'll also make you a better person overall.

The women in your life don't want you to become someone else. They want you to become the best version of who you already are. And that journey starts with understanding that the great mystery of what women want isn't actually that mysterious at all.

It's about being a genuine, emotionally intelligent, respectful human being who can form real connections with other human beings.

Simple? Yes. Easy? Well, that's what the rest of this book is for.

Let's get started.

I

Foundation - Understanding the Basics

1

Throwing Out the Playbook

Mike thought he had it figured out. He'd read the articles, watched the YouTube videos, and memorized the "rules." Wait three days before texting. Always pay for dinner but don't be too eager about it. Be confident but not cocky. Show interest but don't seem desperate. Make her laugh but don't try too hard.

After six months of following this elaborate playbook, Mike had gone on approximately fifteen first dates and exactly zero second dates.

"I don't get it," he told me over coffee, genuinely frustrated. "I'm doing everything I'm supposed to do. I'm being the guy they say women want."

That was his problem right there.

The Playbook Industry

Somewhere along the way, understanding women became an industry. Books, courses, seminars, and YouTube channels all promising to crack the code, reveal the secrets, and give you the magic formula for romantic success. The problem is, most of this advice treats relationships like a video game where you input the right combination of moves and get the desired outcome.

But women aren't video games. They're people.

The playbook approach fails for several fundamental reasons that we need to understand before we can move forward.

Why the Rules Don't Work

They're based on stereotypes, not individuals. The classic dating advice assumes all women respond the same way to the same stimuli. In reality, what attracts one woman might completely turn off another. Sarah might love a guy who's a little mysterious, while Jessica finds that same behavior frustrating and wants straightforward communication.

They focus on tactics instead of character. Most dating advice is about what to do, not who to be. It's about manipulating situations rather than developing the qualities that make you genuinely attractive as a person. You can memorize pickup lines all day, but if you're not actually interesting, funny, or emotionally available, the lines won't save you.

They create inauthentic interactions. When you're following a script, you're not being yourself. And here's the thing about scripts: they're easy to spot. Women have been dealing with men following dating playbooks for decades. They can smell a rehearsed approach from a mile away, and it's usually an immediate turnoff.

They set up adversarial dynamics. The playbook mentality treats dating like a competition where you need to "win" the woman. This creates a dynamic where you're trying to outsmart or manipulate rather than connect. Real relationships are built on collaboration, not conquest.

The Myth of the Alpha Male

Let's talk about one of the most persistent and damaging pieces of dating advice: the idea that women are naturally attracted to "alpha males."

This concept, borrowed from outdated animal behavior research (that has since been debunked even for wolves), suggests that women are hardwired to want dominant, aggressive men who don't show vulnerability or emotion.

Here's what actual research tells us about what women find attractive in long-term partners:

Emotional intelligence ranks consistently higher than dominance. Studies show that women value men who can understand and manage emotions, both their own and others'.

Kindness and empathy are more attractive than aggression. Research from multiple universities consistently shows that kindness is one of the most desired traits in a romantic partner.

Vulnerability, when appropriate, increases attraction. Contrary to the "never show weakness" advice, studies indicate that men who can appropriately share their feelings and admit mistakes are seen as more trustworthy and attractive.

Cooperation is sexier than competition. Women consistently rate men who work well with others and can collaborate effectively as more desirable partners.

The "alpha male" myth persists because it appeals to men who want simple answers and because it's been heavily marketed by people selling courses and books. But it's built on a fundamental misunderstanding of both animal behavior and human psychology.

What Actually Works: The Research

Instead of relying on pickup artist folklore, let's look at what decades of relationship research actually tells us about successful partnerships:

Gottman's research on thousands of couples shows that the most successful relationships are built on friendship, admiration, and turning toward each other during conflict rather than away.

Attachment theory research demonstrates that secure attachment styles, characterized by emotional availability and consistent responsiveness, lead to more satisfying relationships.

Studies on attractiveness consistently show that while physical appearance matters for initial attraction, personality traits like humor, intelligence, and emotional stability become much more important for lasting relationships.

Long-term relationship studies reveal that couples who stay together and report high satisfaction share common traits: they communicate well, show appreciation for each other, maintain physical and emotional intimacy, and support each other's individual growth.

Notice what's not on that list? Game-playing, dominance displays, or emotional manipulation.

The Nice Guy Problem

Now, before you think I'm advocating for becoming a pushover, let's address the "nice guy" issue. Many men have heard that being too nice doesn't work, and they're not entirely wrong. But they're misunderstanding what the problem actually is.

The issue isn't niceness itself. The problem is:

Niceness without boundaries. Being agreeable to the point where you have no opinions or preferences of your own isn't attractive. It's exhausting.

Niceness as a strategy. When you're being nice primarily to get something in return, it comes across as manipulative, not genuine.

Niceness without confidence. If your kindness comes from a place of insecurity or fear of conflict, it doesn't feel authentic.

Niceness without substance. Being pleasant but boring, agreeable but passive, nice but forgettable is a recipe for platonic friendships, not romantic relationships.

The solution isn't to become less nice. It's to become genuinely nice while also being confident, interesting, and authentic.

What Women Actually Respond To

Based on extensive research and countless conversations, here's what consistently attracts women to men:

Genuine confidence - not arrogance or bravado, but the quiet self-assurance that comes from knowing who you are and being comfortable with it.

Emotional intelligence - the ability to understand and manage your own emotions while being attuned to others' feelings.

Authenticity - being genuinely yourself rather than performing a character you think women want to see.

Reliability - following through on what you say you'll do, being consistent in your behavior and treatment of others.

Growth mindset - showing that you're capable of learning, changing, and improving rather than being defensive or stuck in your ways.

Sense of humor - not just making jokes, but being able to find joy and lightness in life while still taking important things seriously.

Respect - treating women as equals, listening to what they say, and valuing their thoughts and feelings.

Real-World Example: David's Transformation

David came to this realization the hard way. For two years, he followed every dating rule he could find. He calculated exactly how long to wait before texting, practiced conversation openers in the mirror, and maintained what he thought was the perfect balance of interest and aloofness.

His dating life was a disaster.

The turning point came when he met Emma at a friend's party. Instead of deploying his usual routine, he was just... himself. He was tired of the games and decided to have genuine conversations. He asked her about her work because he was actually curious, not because he'd read that showing interest was attractive. When she mentioned loving hiking, he didn't pretend to be outdoorsy; instead, he honestly said he was more of an indoor person but would love to hear about her favorite trails.

They talked for three hours.

"The crazy thing," David told me later, "was that it was so much easier than all the strategic stuff I'd been trying. I didn't have to remember what persona I was supposed to be. I could just... talk to her like a human being."

They've been together for two years now.

Common Playbook Mistakes

Let's identify some specific behaviors that need to go:

The three-day rule. This arbitrary waiting period was invented in an era before smartphones and social media. Today, it just comes across as game-playing or disinterest.

Neg-ging. Offering backhanded compliments or subtle insults to "keep her interested" is manipulative and mean-spirited. It doesn't work on women with healthy self-esteem.

The scarcity principle. Acting like you're too busy or important to be available creates distance, not attraction. While you shouldn't be desperate or clingy, artificial scarcity just seems childish.

Performance masculinity. Constantly trying to prove how tough, successful, or alpha you are is exhausting for everyone involved and typically backfires.

The provider audition. Immediately trying to demonstrate your financial worth through expensive dates or gifts can attract the wrong people for the wrong reasons.

Building Your New Approach

So what do you do instead? Here's your new framework:

Be genuinely curious about her as a person. Ask questions because you want to know the answers, not because you're following a conversation script.

Share authentic parts of yourself. This doesn't mean trauma-dumping on the first date, but it does mean being real about your interests, opinions, and experiences.

Respond naturally to her energy. If she texts you and you want to respond, respond. If she seems excited about something, match her enthusiasm if you genuinely feel it.

Focus on connection, not conquest. The goal isn't to "get" her; it's to see if you genuinely connect and enjoy each other's company.

Trust the process. Good relationships develop naturally when two compatible people are authentic with each other. You don't need to force or manipulate the outcome.

The Mindset Shift

The biggest change you need to make isn't in your behavior; it's in your mindset. Stop thinking about dating as something you need to win and start thinking about it as a process of finding someone you genuinely connect with.

This means:

- Some women won't be interested in you, and that's perfectly fine
- You won't be interested in every woman you meet, and that's also fine
- Rejection isn't a reflection of your worth as a person
- The right person will appreciate your authentic self
- You don't need to be perfect to be worthy of love and partnership

Moving Forward

Throwing out the playbook doesn't mean winging it completely. It means replacing artificial strategies with genuine development. Instead of learning pickup lines, work on becoming more interesting. Instead of practicing manufactured confidence, build real self-assurance through personal growth and achievement.

The following chapters will help you develop the actual skills that create lasting attraction and successful relationships. But it all starts here, with the decision to show up as your authentic self rather than performing a character you think women want to see.

Key Takeaways

- Dating advice that treats women like puzzles to be solved is fundamentally flawed
- The "alpha male" concept is based on debunked research and creates toxic relationship dynamics
- Women are attracted to genuine confidence, emotional intelligence, and authenticity
- Being nice isn't the problem; being nice without boundaries, substance, or confidence is
- The goal of dating should be connection, not conquest
- Authenticity is both more effective and much easier than following artificial rules

Action Steps

1. **Identify your playbook behaviors.** Write down the dating "rules" you've been following. Be honest about which ones feel inauthentic or manipulative.
2. **Practice authentic conversation.** In your next social interactions (not necessarily romantic ones), focus on genuine curiosity and honest sharing rather than performing.
3. **Examine your motivations.** Before your next date or interaction with a woman you're interested in, ask yourself: "Am I trying to impress her or connect with her?"
4. **Stop timing your responses.** If you want to text someone, text them. If you don't, don't. Let your genuine interest level guide your communication frequency.

The playbook promised you control, but what it actually gave you was anxiety and artificial interactions. Real attraction and genuine connections come from showing up as your authentic self and treating the women in your life as the complex, interesting individuals they are.

Ready to try something that actually works?

2

The Emotional Intelligence Gap

"I can't read her mind!"

If I had a dollar for every time a man said this to me, I could retire tomorrow. The thing is, most of the time, you don't need to read anyone's mind. The information is usually right there, spoken directly or communicated clearly through behavior. The problem isn't that women are speaking in code; it's that many men haven't developed the skills to pick up on emotional communication.

This isn't your fault, by the way. Most men weren't taught emotional literacy growing up. You learned to throw a ball, change a tire, and maybe balance a checkbook, but nobody sat you down and taught you how to recognize emotional states, validate feelings, or navigate the subtle dynamics of emotional communication.

But here's the thing: it's learnable. And it might be the single most important skill you can develop for your relationships.

What Emotional Intelligence Actually Is

Emotional Intelligence (EI) isn't about becoming overly emotional or losing your rational thinking. It's about four key abilities:

Self-awareness: Understanding your own emotions, what triggers them, and how they affect your behavior.

Self-regulation: Managing your emotional responses appropriately, not being controlled by your feelings but not suppressing them either.

Social awareness: Picking up on other people's emotions and understanding how your behavior affects them.

Relationship management: Using your understanding of emotions to build better connections and handle conflicts constructively.

Think of emotional intelligence as a language. Most men are fluent in the language of facts, solutions, and logic. Many women are bilingual in both logical and emotional communication. When you only speak one language and she's speaking the other, of course you're going to have communication breakdowns.

The Male Emotional Education Gap

Let's be honest about how most men were raised. From early childhood, you probably heard messages like:

- "Boys don't cry"
- "Man up"
- "Don't be so sensitive"
- "Just deal with it"
- "Stop being emotional"

Meanwhile, many girls were encouraged to identify and express their emotions, to talk about feelings, and to pay attention to the emotional climate of their relationships.

This created what researchers call "emotional labor inequality." Women often end up doing the emotional work in relationships because they were trained to do it, while men were trained to suppress or ignore emotional information.

The result? Many men enter adult relationships with underdeveloped emotional skills, then feel frustrated when their partners expect them to operate on an emotional level they've never been taught to access.

Why This Matters in Relationships

Jessica put it perfectly during one of our interviews: "I don't need him to be emotional in the same way I am, but I need him to understand that emotions are information. When I'm upset about something, I'm not just being dramatic. There's usually something important happening that needs attention."

Here's what happens when there's an emotional intelligence gap:

Miscommunication becomes the norm. She says she's "fine" but clearly isn't, and you take her at face value instead of recognizing the emotional subtext.

Problems don't get resolved. You offer solutions when she needs emotional support, or you dismiss feelings as "irrational" instead of understanding what they're communicating.

Intimacy suffers. Without emotional connection, physical and intellectual connection becomes harder to maintain.

She feels alone in the relationship. If you can't connect with her emotionally, she'll feel like she's handling all the emotional labor by herself.

You feel constantly confused. Without emotional literacy, her reactions seem unpredictable and her needs seem impossible to meet.

Real-World Example: The Birthday Disaster

Mark thought he nailed his girlfriend Sarah's birthday. He made reservations at an expensive restaurant, bought her a beautiful necklace, and planned every detail. But during dinner, Sarah seemed off. Not angry exactly, but distant and a little sad.

"What's wrong?" Mark asked. "Do you not like the restaurant?"

"It's fine," Sarah said, but her body language said otherwise.

Mark pressed: "The necklace? I kept the receipt if you want to exchange it."

"No, it's beautiful. Really."

Mark felt frustrated. He'd done everything right, spent a lot of money, planned a perfect evening. Why wasn't she happy?

What Mark missed: Sarah had been dropping hints for weeks about wanting a quiet birthday this year. She'd mentioned feeling overwhelmed at work and looking forward to just staying in together. She'd even shown him a Pinterest board of cozy date ideas.

The expensive dinner and fancy jewelry were lovely, but they communicated that Mark hadn't been listening to what she actually wanted. What felt like thoughtfulness to him felt like inattention to her.

"I felt like he planned the birthday he thought I should want instead of the birthday I actually wanted," Sarah explained later. "It made me feel like he doesn't really know me."

The Three Levels of Emotional Communication

To develop your emotional intelligence, you need to understand that people communicate emotions on three levels:

Level 1: Direct verbal communication: "I'm frustrated with my boss." This is the easiest level. She's telling you exactly what she's feeling and why.

Level 2: Indirect verbal communication: "I'm fine" (said with a sigh and while avoiding eye contact) "It's no big deal" (said in a flat tone) "Whatever you want to do" (said without enthusiasm)

Here, the words say one thing but the tone, timing, and body language say something else. You need to pay attention to the whole message, not just the words.

Level 3: Non-verbal communication:

- Changes in energy level
- Different body language
- Withdrawal or increased distance
- Changes in routine or behavior

This level requires the most skill to read, but it's often where the most important information gets communicated.

Developing Emotional Awareness

Start with yourself. You can't understand others' emotions if you don't understand your own. Begin paying attention to your feelings throughout the day. Instead of just noticing "I feel bad," try to identify specific emotions: frustrated, disappointed, overwhelmed, anxious.

Learn the emotion vocabulary. Most people use about ten emotional words regularly (happy, sad, angry, excited, etc.). Expand your vocabulary. Are you annoyed, irritated, or enraged? Are you content, delighted, or ecstatic? Precision helps.

Notice your emotional triggers. What situations consistently produce strong emotional reactions in you? Understanding your patterns helps you manage them better and helps you understand that others have patterns too.

Practice the pause. When you feel a strong emotion rising, take a breath before reacting. Ask yourself: "What am I actually feeling right now? What's causing this feeling? What would be a helpful response?"

Reading Emotional Cues

Pay attention to changes. If she's usually chatty but becomes quiet, that's information. If she's typically decisive but starts saying "I don't care" about everything, pay attention.

Listen for emotional subtext. When she says "I had lunch with my sister today," is there frustration in her voice? Excitement? Anxiety? The emotion often tells you more than the facts.

Watch body language. Crossed arms, avoiding eye contact, changes in posture, fidgeting, or sudden stillness all communicate emotional states.

Notice energy shifts. Is her energy different than usual? More flat? More intense? More scattered?

Trust your instincts. If something feels off, it probably is. Don't ignore your gut feeling that something's wrong just because she says she's fine.

The Art of Emotional Validation

This might be the most important skill in this chapter. Validation doesn't mean agreeing with everything she feels or thinks. It means acknowledging that her emotions are real and understandable.

Bad validation attempts:

- "You shouldn't feel that way"
- "That's not a big deal"
- "You're overreacting"
- "Just think positive"

- "At least it wasn't worse"

Good validation:

- "That sounds really frustrating"
- "I can see why you'd be upset about that"
- "That must have been hard for you"
- "Your feelings make sense to me"
- "I understand why that would hurt"

Here's the key: you're not validating the situation; you're validating her emotional response to the situation. Even if you would react differently, her feelings are still valid.

When Emotions Seem Irrational

Sometimes her emotional response will seem disproportionate to the situation. Your neighbor borrowed your lawnmower without asking, and you're mildly annoyed. She's genuinely angry about it. Your instinct might be to tell her she's overreacting.

Don't.

Instead, try to understand what the situation represents to her. Maybe it's not really about the lawnmower. Maybe it's about respect, boundaries, or feeling like your shared space isn't being protected. Maybe she's had a bad day and this was the last straw.

Ask questions: "Help me understand why this is so upsetting to you." "What does this situation mean to you?" "Is there more going on here?"

Often, what seems like an overreaction to a small incident is actually a normal reaction to a bigger issue.

The Solution Trap

Men are typically great problem-solvers. When someone presents a problem, your instinct is to fix it. But here's what many men don't realize: sometimes she's not looking for solutions. Sometimes she needs emotional support first.

When she says: "I had the worst day at work. My boss was being unreasonable, the project is falling apart, and I feel like I can't do anything right."

Your instinct might be: "Have you talked to HR about your boss? Maybe you should update your resume. What if you approached the project differently?"

What she might actually need: "That sounds incredibly stressful. I'm sorry you're dealing with all that."

How do you know which she needs? Ask. "Do you want me to help you think through some solutions, or do you just need me to listen right now?"

Most of the time, she'll appreciate being asked. And often, after she feels heard and supported, she'll be more open to problem-solving together.

Emotional Labor and Mental Load

Here's a concept that will revolutionize your understanding of relationships: emotional labor.

Emotional labor is the work of managing emotions in relationships. It includes things like:

- Remembering important dates and events
- Noticing when someone is upset and checking in
- Managing social relationships (remembering to call your mom,

sending holiday cards)
· Keeping track of household needs and family schedules
· Mediating conflicts
· Providing emotional support

In many relationships, women end up doing a disproportionate amount of this work. Not because they're naturally better at it, but because they were trained to do it and men often weren't.

The mental load is the invisible work of keeping track of everything that needs to be done. It's not just doing the dishes; it's remembering that the dishes need to be done, noticing when you're running low on dish soap, and adding dish soap to the grocery list.

When women talk about feeling overwhelmed or unsupported, they're often talking about carrying too much of the emotional labor and mental load.

Practical Emotional Intelligence Exercises

Daily Emotion Check-ins: Twice a day, ask yourself: "What am I feeling right now? What caused this feeling?" Start building your emotional awareness.

The Empathy Exercise: When someone shares something with you, before responding, ask yourself: "How would I feel if I were in their situation?" This builds your ability to see from other perspectives.

Non-verbal Observation: For one week, pay special attention to non-verbal communication. Notice tone of voice, body language, and energy levels in your interactions.

The Validation Practice: When someone expresses a feeling, practice validating it before offering advice or solutions. "That sounds frustrating" before "Have you tried..."

Emotional Labor Audit: Look at your relationship and honestly assess who's doing what emotional and mental work. Are you carrying your fair share?

Common Emotional Intelligence Mistakes

Assuming logic always trumps emotion. Both are important. Emotions often contain valuable information that pure logic misses.

Trying to talk her out of feelings. You can't reason someone out of an emotion. You can help them process it and understand it.

Taking her emotions personally. Her frustration about work isn't about you, even if she's less available or more irritable at home because of it.

Expecting her to manage your emotions for you. Your emotional well-being is your responsibility. She can support you, but she can't fix your emotional problems.

Avoiding emotional conversations. The more you practice, the easier they become. Avoidance just makes the skill harder to develop.

Building Your Emotional Intelligence

Read about emotions. Learn about different types of emotions, what causes them, and how they function.

Practice mindfulness. Being present in the moment helps you notice emotional information you might otherwise miss.

Ask questions. When you're not sure what someone is feeling, ask. "How are you feeling about that?" "What's that like for you?"

Reflect on your relationships. Think about past relationship conflicts. Were there emotional dynamics you missed? What could you have done differently?

Get comfortable with feelings. Yours and others'. They're not dangerous or irrational. They're information.

The Long-term Benefits

Developing emotional intelligence isn't just about understanding women better. It will improve every relationship in your life and make you a more effective person overall. Men with higher emotional intelligence report:

- Better relationships with romantic partners, friends, and family
- Greater success in leadership roles
- Less stress and better mental health
- More satisfying social connections
- Better conflict resolution skills

It's not about becoming more emotional. It's about becoming more emotionally intelligent. There's a big difference.

Key Takeaways

- Emotional intelligence is a learnable skill set, not a personality trait
- Many men weren't taught emotional literacy, creating a gap in relationship skills
- Emotions are information, not obstacles to overcome with logic
- Validation means acknowledging feelings are real and understandable
- Sometimes people need emotional support before practical solutions
- Emotional labor and mental load should be shared fairly in relationships
- Developing emotional intelligence benefits every area of your life

Action Steps

1. **Start an emotion journal.** For one week, write down what you're feeling twice a day and what might have caused those feelings.
2. **Practice active listening.** In your next conversation with someone who's sharing something emotional, focus on understanding their feelings before offering advice.
3. **Ask the magic question.** Next time someone shares a problem with you, ask: "Do you want me to help brainstorm solutions, or do you just need me to listen?"
4. **Do an emotional labor inventory.** List all the emotional and mental tasks in your relationships. Are you carrying your fair share?
5. **Practice validation.** For one week, focus on validating people's feelings before responding with your own thoughts or advice.

Emotional intelligence isn't about becoming more sensitive or losing your ability to think logically. It's about adding another layer of awareness that will make you more effective in every relationship you have.

The women in your life aren't complicated or mysterious. They're just communicating on a level you might not have been taught to access. Once you develop these skills, you'll wonder how you ever functioned without them.

3

She's Not Your Mother (Or Your Therapist)

"I feel like I'm dating a teenager."

Rachel said this to me about her boyfriend of eight months, and the frustration in her voice was unmistakable. "He's 32 years old, but I have to remind him to do laundry, tell him when we're running low on groceries, and manage his social calendar because he 'forgets' to respond to his friends. Last week, I had to call his doctor to reschedule his appointment because he kept putting it off."

She paused, then added: "I wanted a partner, not another person to take care of."

If this stings a little, good. It means you're paying attention.

One of the biggest relationship killers is when romantic partners slip into parent-child dynamics. And unfortunately, due to a combination of how many men were raised and societal expectations, men often end up in the "child" role without even realizing it.

This chapter is about recognizing those patterns and building the self-sufficiency that makes you an attractive partner rather than a burden.

The Mothering Trap

Here's how it typically happens: You meet someone amazing. She's caring, nurturing, and naturally notices when things need to be done. She starts picking up some slack here and there—reminding you about your dentist appointment, buying groceries when you forget, doing your laundry when you run out of clean clothes.

At first, it feels great. Someone cares about you! Someone's looking out for you! You feel loved and taken care of.

But what you've actually created is an unhealthy dynamic where she's functioning as your caretaker rather than your equal partner. And eventually, she's going to resent it. Not because she doesn't love you, but because romantic relationships should be partnerships between two adults, not one adult taking care of another.

How This Pattern Develops

The Learned Helplessness Factor: Many men grew up in households where their mothers handled most of the domestic and emotional labor. They never learned to notice when milk was running low or when social relationships needed tending. They learned to wait for someone else to handle these things.

The Different Standards Problem: Research shows that men and women often have different standards for cleanliness, organization, and social maintenance. When you don't notice something needs to be done, she often ends up doing it rather than letting it slide.

The Mental Load Inequality: As we discussed in the previous chapter, someone has to keep track of what needs to be done, when it needs to happen, and who's responsible for it. When that person is always her, she becomes the manager of your life rather than your partner in it.

The Emotional Labor Imbalance: She becomes responsible not just for her own emotional well-being, but for managing yours too, mediating your conflicts, and maintaining your social relationships.

Real-World Example: Tom and Lisa's Wake-Up Call

Tom thought he was a good boyfriend. He worked hard, was faithful, and genuinely loved Lisa. But after two years together, she seemed increasingly frustrated with him, and he couldn't figure out why.

The breaking point came during a conversation about moving in together.

"I don't think I'm ready," Lisa said.

"Why? I thought we were happy."

"Tom, in the two years we've been together, have you ever planned a date? Like, actually researched restaurants, made reservations, thought about what I might enjoy?"

Tom thought about it. "Well, no, but you're so much better at that stuff..."

"Have you ever remembered my friends' names without me reminding you? Sent a birthday card to your own family members? Noticed when your apartment was running low on food or toilet paper?"

The list went on. Lisa wasn't asking him to be perfect, but she was asking him to be a functional adult who could manage his own life and contribute equally to their relationship.

"I felt like I was dating someone who needed a mom, not someone who wanted a partner," Lisa explained. "I was constantly managing his life, and it was exhausting."

The relationship ended six months later, not because they didn't love each other, but because the dynamic had become unsustainable.

The Therapist Problem

Beyond the mothering dynamic, there's another equally problematic pattern: treating your romantic partner as your personal therapist. This looks like:

- Making her responsible for managing your emotional states
- Expecting her to solve your personal problems
- Using her as your only source of emotional support
- Dumping all your stress and anxiety on her without considering her capacity
- Expecting her to validate and soothe all your insecurities

Here's the thing: healthy relationships involve emotional support, but they should be reciprocal. If she's always giving support and you're always receiving it, that's not a partnership—that's therapy.

The Attraction Killer

Why does this dynamic destroy attraction? Because attraction is built on seeing someone as your equal. When you're functioning as someone's child or patient, they stop seeing you as a potential romantic and sexual partner.

Competence is attractive. Women are attracted to men who can handle their own lives, solve their own problems, and contribute meaningfully to a partnership.

Independence is sexy. Knowing that you're choosing to be with her, rather than needing her to function, makes the relationship feel more secure and desirable.

Reciprocity builds intimacy. When both people are giving and receiving support, care, and effort, it creates a positive cycle that strengthens the relationship.

Respect requires equality. It's hard to maintain romantic respect for someone you have to parent or constantly rescue.

Signs You Might Be in This Pattern

Be honest with yourself. Do any of these sound familiar?

Domestic Life:

- She reminds you about appointments, deadlines, or commitments
- She does more than her share of household management
- You "help" with housework rather than taking equal responsibility
- She's the one who notices when things need to be bought, fixed, or cleaned
- You wait for her to plan social activities or date nights

Emotional Dynamics:

- She's always the one providing comfort when you're stressed
- You rarely ask how she's feeling or offer support for her problems
- She mediates conflicts between you and other people
- You rely on her to manage your relationships with friends or family
- She's your primary or only emotional support system

Financial and Practical Matters:

- She handles most of the logistical planning in your relationship
- You defer to her on most decisions, then complain if you don't like the outcomes
- She manages your social calendar or reminds you about social obligations

- You expect her to know your schedule and preferences without communicating them

Personal Growth:

- You expect her to motivate you to pursue your goals
- She's more invested in your success than you are
- You rely on her to point out your problems rather than being self-aware
- You expect her to change or adapt to accommodate your shortcomings

Building Self-Sufficiency

The goal isn't to become completely independent—healthy relationships involve interdependence. The goal is to become a fully functional adult who can contribute equally to a partnership.

Practical Self-Sufficiency

Learn basic life skills. If you can't cook, clean, do laundry, manage a calendar, or handle basic household maintenance, learn. These aren't "women's work"—they're adult responsibilities.

Develop your own systems. Don't rely on her to remember your appointments, deadlines, or commitments. Use whatever tools work for you—phone calendars, reminders, apps, notebooks.

Take initiative. Don't wait to be asked or reminded. Notice what needs to be done and do it. See that you're running low on groceries? Make a list and go shopping.

Plan things. Take responsibility for planning dates, social activities, or trips sometimes. Show that you're invested in creating positive experiences together.

Handle your own relationships. Maintain your friendships, remember important dates for your family members, handle your own conflicts. She shouldn't have to manage your social life.

Emotional Self-Sufficiency

Develop multiple sources of support. Friends, family, mentors, therapists, support groups—don't make her your only emotional outlet.

Learn to self-soothe. Develop healthy ways to manage stress, anxiety, and difficult emotions that don't require her constant intervention.

Take responsibility for your mental health. If you struggle with depression, anxiety, or other mental health issues, get professional help rather than expecting her to manage your symptoms.

Practice emotional reciprocity. Ask about her day, her feelings, her challenges. Offer support and comfort when she needs it.

Become self-aware. Notice your own patterns, triggers, and areas for growth without needing her to point them out.

The Partnership Model

Instead of a parent-child or therapist-patient dynamic, aim for a partnership model:

Shared responsibility. Both people contribute to household management, emotional labor, and relationship maintenance.

Mutual support. Both people give and receive comfort, encouragement, and help.

Individual competence. Both people can function independently but choose to share their lives.

Reciprocal care. Both people notice and respond to each other's needs.

Equal investment. Both people are equally committed to the relationship's success and growth.

Real-World Example: Marcus's Transformation

Marcus realized he had a problem when his girlfriend Sarah made a comment about feeling like his "life manager." Initially, he was defensive. He worked hard, he contributed financially, he was loyal—what more did she want?

But when he really looked at their dynamic, he saw her point. Sarah planned their dates, managed their social calendar, reminded him about appointments, and even handled most of the communication with his own family.

Instead of getting defensive, Marcus decided to change. He started small:

- He took over planning one date night per month
- He set up his own calendar system and stopped relying on Sarah's reminders
- He started checking in with his parents and siblings directly
- He began noticing household tasks that needed doing rather than waiting to be asked

"The crazy thing," Marcus told me later, "was how much better I felt about myself. I didn't realize how much I had been depending on Sarah to function. When I started handling my own life, I felt more confident and capable."

Sarah noticed too. "It was like dating a different person," she said. "Not completely different, but more... adult. More like an equal partner."

The Transition Period

Changing these patterns can be challenging, especially if they've been established for a while. Here's how to navigate the transition:

Start small. Pick one area and focus on taking full responsibility for it. Maybe it's managing your own calendar, or planning date nights, or handling your own laundry.

Communicate about the changes. Let her know you're working on being more self-sufficient. This helps her understand what's happening and gives her permission to step back.

Expect some resistance. If she's been managing certain aspects of your life for a long time, it might feel strange for both of you when you start handling them yourself.

Be consistent. Don't take on new responsibilities and then abandon them after a few weeks. Follow through on your commitments.

Ask for feedback. "How am I doing with taking more initiative around the house?" "Do you feel like I'm contributing more equally to our relationship?"

Common Pushback and How to Handle It

"But she's better at that stuff." Maybe she is, but that doesn't mean you can't learn or shouldn't contribute. Being "worse" at something isn't an excuse to never do it.

"She doesn't mind doing it." She might not complain, but that doesn't mean the imbalance isn't affecting the relationship. Many women don't feel comfortable directly asking their partners to be more self-sufficient.

"I work long hours, so she handles more at home." Working outside the home doesn't exempt you from all domestic and emotional responsibilities, especially if she also works.

"We have different standards." Then you need to negotiate what reasonable standards look like for both of you, not simply defer to her to handle everything to her standards.

The Benefits of Self-Sufficiency

When you become genuinely self-sufficient:

She'll see you differently. You'll go from being someone she takes care of to someone she partners with.

You'll feel more confident. Managing your own life successfully builds genuine self-esteem.

The relationship becomes more balanced. Both people are contributing equally, which reduces resentment and increases satisfaction.

Attraction increases. Competence and independence are genuinely attractive qualities.

You become more resilient. If the relationship ended (which is less likely when it's healthy), you'd be able to function on your own.

Advanced Partnership Skills

Once you've mastered basic self-sufficiency, you can work on advanced partnership skills:

Anticipating needs. Noticing what needs to be done before being asked.

Emotional attunement. Recognizing when she needs support and offering it.

Shared decision-making. Taking equal responsibility for major decisions and their consequences.

Future planning. Being equally invested in long-term goals and planning.

Conflict resolution. Taking responsibility for your part in disagreements and working toward solutions.

When Professional Help Is Needed

Sometimes the patterns run so deep that you need professional support to change them. Consider couples therapy or individual therapy if:

- You've tried to change these patterns but keep falling back into them
- She's expressed that she feels more like a parent than a partner
- You realize you have significant emotional dependence issues
- The relationship is suffering despite your efforts to change

Key Takeaways

- Romantic relationships should be partnerships between equals, not caretaking arrangements
- Many men inadvertently slip into child-like roles in relationships due to learned helplessness
- Self-sufficiency in practical and emotional matters is essential for healthy relationships
- Competence and independence are attractive qualities that strengthen relationships
- Both partners should contribute equally to household, emotional, and relationship management
- Changing these patterns requires consistent effort and may feel uncomfortable at first
- Professional help is available if you're struggling to make these changes on your own

Action Steps

1. **Conduct an honest assessment.** List all the ways your partner currently manages your life or provides caretaking. Be brutally honest.
2. **Pick three areas to change.** Choose three specific responsibilities you'll take over completely. Start with manageable ones.
3. **Create your own systems.** Set up whatever tools you need to manage your calendar, remember appointments, track household needs, etc.
4. **Plan something.** Take complete responsibility for planning your next date or social activity.
5. **Build your support network.** Identify at least two people besides your partner who you can talk to when you need emotional support.
6. **Have the conversation.** Talk to your partner about these changes. Ask for feedback and be open to hearing about areas you might not have recognized.

Remember, the goal isn't to become completely independent. The goal is to become an equal partner who contributes to the relationship rather than someone who needs to be managed within it.

When both people in a relationship are fully functioning adults who choose to share their lives, that's when the real magic happens. That's when you move from a caretaking dynamic to a true partnership built on mutual respect, attraction, and genuine love.

You're not looking for someone to take care of you. You're looking for someone to build a life with. Make sure you're showing up as someone who can actually build, not just someone who needs to be taken care of.

II

Communication - The Real Game Changer

4

Listen Like Your Relationship Depends On It (Because It Does)

"He hears me, but he doesn't listen to me."

This is one of the most common complaints women have about their partners. And before you roll your eyes and think this is about women being too demanding or emotional, let me share some research that might surprise you.

Dr. John Gottman, who has studied thousands of couples over decades, found that the number one predictor of relationship success isn't compatibility, shared interests, or even attraction. It's the quality of communication between partners. And at the heart of good communication is one skill that most people think they already have but actually need to develop: listening.

Real listening. Not just waiting for your turn to talk, not just collecting facts, and definitely not just nodding along while you think about other things. We're talking about the kind of listening that makes people feel truly heard and understood.

The Listening Illusion

Here's the uncomfortable truth: most of us are terrible listeners. We think we're good at it because we can repeat back what someone said, but that's only one small part of real listening.

Consider this scenario: Your girlfriend comes home from work and says, "I had the worst day. My boss was completely unreasonable about the Morrison project, Sarah didn't pull her weight again, and I feel like I'm drowning in deadlines."

Surface-level listening captures the facts: bad day, difficult boss, problematic coworker, too much work.

Real listening also picks up on: the frustration in her voice, the fact that she feels unsupported at work, that she might be questioning her competence ("I'm drowning"), and that she might need some emotional support right now.

Most men hear the first part. The second part requires skills that many of us were never taught.

Why Men Often Struggle With Listening

Let's be honest about some of the barriers:

We're socialized to solve problems. When someone presents a problem, our instinct is to jump to solutions rather than fully understanding the emotional experience.

We focus on facts over feelings. We're trained to prioritize logical information over emotional information, which means we miss half of what people are actually communicating.

We get uncomfortable with emotions. Many men weren't taught to sit comfortably with emotional experiences, so we rush to "fix" them rather than simply being present with them.

We assume understanding. Because men often communicate more directly, we sometimes assume that what women say is all they mean, missing the emotional subtext.

We're distracted. We try to multitask during conversations, checking our phones or thinking about other things while someone is talking.

The Cost of Poor Listening

When you don't listen well, here's what happens in your relationships:

She feels unheard and misunderstood. This creates distance and resentment over time.

Problems don't get resolved. If you don't fully understand what's wrong, you can't help fix it or support her through it.

Intimacy decreases. People share their inner worlds with those who truly listen. When you don't listen well, she'll stop sharing as much.

Conflicts escalate. Misunderstandings multiply when people don't feel heard, leading to bigger arguments about smaller issues.

She seeks connection elsewhere. If she doesn't feel heard by you, she'll find other people who listen better.

Real-World Example: The Work Story Disaster

Jake's girlfriend Emma came home upset about a situation with her boss. She'd been passed over for a project she really wanted, and she was questioning whether she was valued at her company.

Here's how Jake listened:

Emma: "I can't believe they gave the Peterson account to Michael. I've been working on client relationships longer than he has, and I know that industry better."

Jake: "Well, maybe Michael has connections you don't know about. Or maybe they're looking at different qualifications. Have you talked to your boss about what you need to do to get the next big account?"

Emma: "That's not the point. It's about respect. I feel like they don't see my contributions."

Jake: "But getting upset about it won't change anything. You should focus on the next opportunity."

Emma: "Never mind. You don't get it."

Jake was confused and frustrated. He'd offered practical advice. He was trying to help. Why was Emma shutting down?

What Jake missed: Emma wasn't looking for solutions in that moment. She was feeling undervalued and wanted Jake to understand how that felt. She needed validation that her disappointment made sense before she could think about next steps.

Here's how the conversation could have gone:

Emma: "I can't believe they gave the Peterson account to Michael…"

Jake: "Wow, that must be really disappointing. You've been working so hard to build those client relationships."

Emma: "Exactly! I feel like they don't even see what I contribute."

Jake: "That has to be incredibly frustrating. You put so much into your work."

Emma: "It is frustrating. I love my job, but sometimes I wonder if they value me."

Jake: "That's a hard feeling to sit with. What do you think you want to do about it?"

In the second version, Jake listened to both the facts and the emotions. He validated her feelings before moving toward solutions. As a result, Emma felt heard and could think more clearly about her options.

The Four Levels of Listening

Level 1: Distracted Listening

You're physically present but mentally elsewhere. You might catch some words, but you miss most of the content and all of the emotional information.

Level 2: Surface Listening

You hear the words and can repeat back the basic facts, but you miss the emotional meaning and subtext.

Level 3: Active Listening

You hear both the content and the emotions. You ask clarifying questions and reflect back what you're hearing.

Level 4: Empathetic Listening

You hear the words, emotions, and underlying needs. You can put yourself in their shoes and understand not just what they're saying, but what they're experiencing.

Most relationships need Level 3 or 4 listening to thrive, but many people operate at Level 1 or 2.

The Components of Real Listening

Full Attention: Put away your phone. Turn off the TV. Make eye contact. Your body language should communicate that this person and this conversation are the most important things in your world right now.

Patience: Don't rush to respond. Let her finish her thoughts completely, including the pauses where she's collecting her thoughts.

Emotional Awareness: Pay attention to tone of voice, body language, and energy level. Often the emotional content is more important than the factual content.

Reflection: Occasionally reflect back what you're hearing: "It sounds like you're feeling really frustrated with how your boss handled that situation."

Clarification: Ask questions that help you understand better: "When you say you feel unsupported, what would support look like to you?"

Validation: Acknowledge that her feelings and experiences are valid and understandable.

Active Listening Techniques

The Mirror Method: "What I'm hearing is..." or "It sounds like you're saying..." This helps ensure you're understanding correctly and shows that you're paying attention.

Emotion Labeling: "That must have been frustrating" or "You sound excited about this." This shows you're picking up on the emotional content, not just the facts.

The Pause: After she finishes talking, count to three before responding. This ensures she's really done and gives you time to process what you heard.

Clarifying Questions: "Help me understand what that was like for you" or "What was the hardest part about that situation?"

The Summary: For longer conversations, occasionally summarize: "Let me make sure I understand everything. You're dealing with X, feeling Y, and you're concerned about Z."

Listening to Different Types of Communication

Venting vs. Problem-Solving: Sometimes she needs to express frustration or disappointment without necessarily wanting solutions. Ask: "Do you want to talk through some options, or do you just need me to listen right now?"

Sharing vs. Seeking Advice: When she shares something positive or exciting, she might just want to share the joy with you. Match her energy and enthusiasm before asking questions or offering thoughts.

Processing vs. Deciding: Sometimes she's thinking out loud, working through her thoughts and feelings. Don't feel pressure to provide answers; just provide a safe space for her to process.

Emotional Dumps vs. Conversations: If she's had a really hard day and needs to download everything, let her get it all out before trying to engage. Sometimes people just need to empty their emotional bucket.

Common Listening Mistakes

The Immediate Solution: Jumping to problem-solving mode before fully understanding the situation and emotions involved.

The Comparison Trap: "That reminds me of when I..." This shifts focus from her experience to yours.

The Minimizer: "It's not that bad" or "At least..." This invalidates her emotional experience.

The Interrogator: Asking so many questions that it feels like a deposition rather than a supportive conversation.

The Multitasker: Trying to listen while doing other things. This communicates that the conversation isn't important enough for your full attention.

The Fixer: Constantly offering advice or solutions instead of just being present with her experience.

The Judge: Evaluating whether her feelings are "reasonable" or "justified" instead of simply accepting them as her reality.

Listening During Conflict

This is where listening becomes most challenging and most important.

Stay Calm: Your emotional state affects your ability to listen. If you're getting defensive or angry, take a breath or ask for a brief pause.

Listen for the Need Behind the Complaint: "You never help with housework" might really mean "I feel unsupported and overwhelmed."

Avoid Defensive Responses: Instead of immediately defending yourself, try to understand why she feels the way she does.

Acknowledge Before Explaining: "I can see why you'd feel that way" before "But here's what I was thinking..."

Ask for Clarification: "Help me understand what you need from me" or "What would feel more supportive to you?"

The Art of the Follow-Up

Good listening doesn't end when the conversation ends.

Check In Later: "How are you feeling about that situation with your boss now?" This shows you were really listening and that you care about her ongoing experience.

Remember Important Details: If she mentioned a big presentation on Thursday, ask about it on Thursday evening. This demonstrates that you truly heard what was important to her.

Notice Patterns: If she's been stressed about work for several weeks, you might say, "It seems like work has been really challenging lately. How are you holding up?"

Take Action When Appropriate: If during your conversation you learned about something you could help with, follow through without being asked.

Building Your Listening Skills

Practice Meditation or Mindfulness: These practices improve your ability to be present and focused during conversations.

Watch Body Language: Practice noticing non-verbal communication in all your interactions, not just romantic ones.

Ask Better Questions: Instead of "How was your day?" try "What was the best part of your day?" or "What was challenging about today?"

Listen to Understand, Not to Respond: Focus on truly comprehending what she's saying rather than formulating your response while she's talking.

Practice with Low-Stakes Conversations: Develop your listening skills with friends, family members, and colleagues before applying them in emotionally charged situations.

Real-World Example: David's Listening Transformation

David realized he had a listening problem when his girlfriend mentioned the same work issue three times in one week, and each time it was like he was hearing it for the first time.

"I was physically present for the conversations," David explained, "but I wasn't really absorbing what she was saying. I was thinking about work, or my fantasy football lineup, or what we should do for dinner."

David started practicing what he called "aggressive listening"—deliberately focusing all his attention on conversations with his girlfriend.

"The first thing I noticed was how much more interesting our conversations became," he said. "When you really listen to someone, you realize how much depth they have, how many interesting thoughts and feelings they experience every day."

His girlfriend noticed too. "It felt like he was actually interested in my inner world for the first time," she said. "Before, I felt like I was talking to someone who was politely waiting for me to finish. Now it feels like he genuinely wants to understand me."

Creating Space for Deep Conversations

Regular Check-ins: Schedule time for real conversations, not just logistical planning or casual chat.

Device-Free Time: Create periods where phones, TVs, and other distractions are off-limits.

Comfortable Environment: Have these conversations somewhere comfortable and private where you won't be interrupted.

Open-Ended Questions: "What's been on your mind lately?" or "How are you feeling about things in general?"

Patience: Sometimes it takes time for people to open up. Don't rush or pressure, just create consistent space for deeper sharing.

The Ripple Effects of Better Listening

When you become a truly good listener:

Intimacy Deepens: People share more of themselves with those who listen well, creating stronger emotional connections.

Conflicts Decrease: When people feel heard, they're less likely to escalate disagreements or repeat the same complaints.

Trust Increases: Being truly listened to builds trust and emotional safety in relationships.

She'll Listen Better Too: Good listening is often reciprocal. When you listen well, others tend to listen better to you.

You'll Understand Her Better: Regular, attentive listening helps you understand her patterns, needs, and inner world more clearly.

Advanced Listening Skills

Reading Between the Lines: Understanding what she's not saying as much as what she is saying.

Emotional Regulation: Managing your own emotional reactions so you can stay present with hers.

Cultural and Individual Context: Understanding how her background, experiences, and personality affect how she communicates.

Timing Awareness: Recognizing when she's ready for deep conversations vs. when she needs space.

Energy Management: Knowing when you're too tired or distracted to listen well and communicating that honestly.

When Listening Isn't Enough

Sometimes, even with excellent listening skills, relationships face challenges that require additional support:

- If the same issues keep coming up despite good communication
- If she seems chronically unhappy or unfulfilled
- If you're having trouble understanding each other despite your best efforts
- If conflicts are escalating rather than resolving

In these cases, couples therapy can provide additional tools and perspectives.

Key Takeaways

- Real listening involves hearing both content and emotions, not just collecting facts
- Many men struggle with listening because they were taught to solve problems rather than understand experiences
- Good listening requires full attention, patience, and emotional awareness
- Validation often matters more than solutions in emotional conversations
- Listening skills can be developed through practice and intentional effort
- The quality of listening in a relationship directly impacts intimacy, trust, and satisfaction
- Following up on conversations shows you truly heard what was

important

Action Steps

1. **Assess Your Current Listening:** For one week, pay attention to how you listen in conversations. Are you fully present? Do you interrupt? Are you thinking about your response while she's talking?
2. **Practice the Three-Second Rule:** After someone finishes talking, count to three before responding. This ensures they're really done and gives you time to process.
3. **Try Reflection Listening:** In your next meaningful conversation, practice reflecting back what you hear: "It sounds like..." or "What I'm hearing is..."
4. **Ask the Magic Question:** When someone shares a problem, ask: "Do you want me to help think through solutions, or do you just need me to listen?"
5. **Remove Distractions:** For one week, put your phone away completely during conversations with your partner.
6. **Follow Up:** Practice remembering and following up on things she tells you. If she mentions a stressful meeting on Tuesday, ask about it Tuesday evening.

Good listening is one of the greatest gifts you can give someone. It says, "You matter to me. Your thoughts and feelings are important. Your inner world is worth my attention."

In a world where everyone is constantly distracted and rushed, being someone who truly listens is incredibly rare and valuable. It's also one of the most attractive qualities you can develop.

The women in your life don't need you to solve all their problems. But they do need to feel heard, understood, and valued. Learning to listen well isn't just about better relationships—it's about becoming the kind of person others feel safe opening up to.

And that's the foundation of every meaningful connection you'll ever have.

5

The Art of the Real Conversation

"We can talk for hours about everything except the things that actually matter."

Amy said this about her relationship with her boyfriend of two years, and it perfectly captures one of the most common relationship problems: couples who are great at surface-level communication but terrible at deeper connection.

They could discuss work schedules, weekend plans, what to have for dinner, and the latest Netflix series. But when it came to fears, dreams, relationship concerns, or deeper emotions, their conversations became awkward, superficial, or non-existent.

If your relationship consists mainly of logistical coordination punctuated by small talk, you're missing out on the kind of deep connection that creates lasting intimacy and attraction.

The Small Talk Trap

Small talk has its place. It's social lubrication, it helps us connect casually, and it can be genuinely enjoyable. The problem isn't small talk itself; the problem is when that's all you have.

Many couples fall into what relationship researchers call the "roommate syndrome"—they function well as household partners and social companions, but they've lost the deeper emotional and intellectual connection that makes them romantic partners.

This happens gradually. Early in relationships, everything feels significant because you're still discovering each other. She mentions she's always wanted to learn Italian, and it's fascinating. Two years later, you barely register when she talks about her day.

But here's the thing: she's still growing, changing, and having new thoughts and experiences every day. If you're not having real conversations, you're not keeping up with who she's becoming.

What Real Conversations Look Like

Real conversations go beyond facts and logistics to explore thoughts, feelings, experiences, and meaning. They create intimacy because they require vulnerability from both people.

Surface conversation: "How was your day?" "Fine. Yours?" "Good. What should we have for dinner?"

Real conversation: "What was the most interesting part of your day?" This opens the door to actual sharing rather than just status updates.

Surface conversation: "Your sister called earlier." "What did she want?" "Just to chat."

Real conversation: "Your sister sounded stressed when she called. How do you think she's really doing with everything going on?" This explores concern, family dynamics, and deeper awareness.

Surface conversation: "We should plan a vacation soon." "Yeah, where do you want to go?" "I don't know, somewhere warm."

Real conversation: "I've been thinking about what kind of experience would feel really rejuvenating for us right now. What do you think we both need most—adventure, relaxation, time to reconnect?" This explores needs, desires, and shared goals.

The Fear of Going Deeper

Why do so many people, especially men, stay on the surface? Several fears often drive this:

Fear of opening a can of worms. "If I ask how she's really feeling about her job, she might talk for an hour about all her workplace frustrations."

Fear of not knowing what to say. "What if she shares something deep and I don't know how to respond appropriately?"

Fear of reciprocal vulnerability. "If I ask her about her fears or dreams, she might ask me about mine, and I'm not ready for that conversation."

Fear of conflict. "What if we discover we disagree about something important?"

Fear of intimacy. Sometimes surface-level communication feels safer than the vulnerability that real intimacy requires.

These fears are understandable, but they're also relationship killers. The very things you're avoiding—vulnerability, emotional depth, potential disagreement—are what create real connection between people.

Real-World Example: Matt and Jennifer's Breakthrough

Matt and Jennifer had been together for three years and were considering engagement, but Jennifer felt like something was missing.

"We get along great," she explained to me. "We have fun together, we handle practical stuff well, but I feel like I don't really know him. I know his preferences and his schedule, but I don't know his dreams or his fears or what really matters to him."

When Matt heard this feedback, his initial reaction was defensive. "We talk all the time! We're always communicating!"

But when he really thought about it, he realized Jennifer was right. Their conversations were mostly about logistics, current events, or shared activities. They rarely talked about anything deeply personal.

The breakthrough came when Jennifer asked him a simple question: "If you could do anything with your life, regardless of money or practical constraints, what would it be?"

Matt's first instinct was to deflect: "I don't know, I haven't really thought about it." But Jennifer waited patiently, and eventually Matt opened up about a dream he'd never shared with anyone: he'd always wanted to teach high school history.

"I've been thinking about it more and more," Matt admitted. "I like my job in marketing fine, but I don't feel like I'm making a difference. I think I'd love teaching."

That conversation led to others about Matt's values, his sense of purpose, his fears about making career changes, and his vision for their future together. It was the beginning of a much deeper connection.

"It was like I finally got to meet the real Matt," Jennifer said later. "I'd been dating the surface version of him for three years."

The Anatomy of Deep Conversations

They start with genuine curiosity. Real conversations begin when you're actually interested in understanding someone's inner world, not just collecting information.

They require patience. People need time to access and articulate deeper thoughts and feelings. You can't rush authentic sharing.

They involve reciprocal vulnerability. Both people share something real about themselves. It's not an interview; it's an exchange.

They explore meaning, not just facts. Instead of just what happened, you explore what it meant, how it felt, what it revealed.

They create emotional safety. People can share without fear of judgment, dismissal, or having their words used against them later.

Topics That Create Connection

Dreams and Aspirations

- "What would you do if you knew you couldn't fail?"
- "What's something you've always wanted to try but haven't yet?"
- "How do you want to be different five years from now?"

Values and Beliefs

- "What's a principle you'd never compromise on?"
- "What does a meaningful life look like to you?"
- "What's something you believe that most people disagree with?"

Fears and Vulnerabilities

- "What's your biggest fear about our relationship?"
- "What's something you worry about that you don't usually talk about?"
- "What's a way you feel vulnerable in your life right now?"

Childhood and Family

- "What's something from your childhood that still affects how you see the world?"
- "What did your parents teach you about relationships that you want

to keep or change?"
· "What's a family tradition you'd like us to start?"

Personal Growth

· "What's something you're learning about yourself lately?"
· "How do you think you've changed in the past few years?"
· "What's a challenge you're facing that's helping you grow?"

Relationship Reflections

· "What do you love most about us as a couple?"
· "What's something I do that makes you feel really loved?"
· "How can we stay connected as life gets busier?"

The Art of Asking Better Questions

The quality of your questions determines the depth of your conversations.

Instead of: "How was work?" **Try:** "What was the most satisfying part of your day?"

Instead of: "Did you have fun with your friends?" **Try:** "What did you and Sarah talk about? How is she doing with everything?"

Instead of: "Are you okay?" **Try:** "You seem quieter than usual tonight. What's on your mind?"

Instead of: "What do you want to do this weekend?" **Try:** "What kind of weekend would feel really good to you right now?"

Instead of: "How do you feel about that?" **Try:** "What was that experience like for you?"

Creating the Right Environment

Deep conversations don't just happen; they need the right conditions:

Remove distractions. Phones away, TV off, somewhere you won't be interrupted.

Choose the right timing. Not when someone is stressed, tired, or distracted. Some people are more open in the evening; others prefer morning conversations.

Start gradually. You don't need to dive into the deepest possible topics immediately. Build up to more vulnerable conversations.

Make it reciprocal. Share something about yourself too. Don't make it feel like an interrogation.

Follow their lead. If she opens up about something, give it the attention it deserves rather than immediately changing topics.

Navigating Difficult Conversations

Sometimes real conversations involve topics that are challenging or emotionally charged.

Relationship Issues: When something isn't working in your relationship, avoiding conversation makes it worse. Approach these talks with curiosity rather than blame: "I've noticed we haven't been as physically affectionate lately. How are you feeling about that?"

Future Planning: Conversations about marriage, children, career moves, or life changes can feel heavy, but they're crucial for long-term compatibility. "I'd love to understand how you picture our life together in the next few years."

Family Dynamics: Her relationship with her family affects your relationship with her. Show genuine interest in understanding these dynamics rather than just tolerating them.

Money and Values: Financial conversations reveal values and priorities. Explore not just the practical aspects but what money represents to each of you.

Past Relationships: While you don't need to know every detail, understanding how past relationships have shaped her can deepen your understanding of who she is and what she needs.

Common Conversation Killers

The Advice Giver: Jumping into solution mode instead of exploring the experience or emotion.

The Topic Jumper: Moving quickly from subject to subject instead of going deeper into any one area.

The Interviewer: Asking question after question without sharing anything about yourself.

The Judge: Responding to vulnerability with criticism or analysis instead of acceptance.

The Deflector: Using humor or topic changes to avoid emotional depth when things get real.

The Phone Checker: Breaking the connection by checking devices during intimate conversations.

Building Emotional Vocabulary

Many people struggle with deep conversations because they don't have the words for complex emotions and experiences. Expanding your emotional vocabulary helps you both understand and express subtlety. Instead of just "good" or "bad," try:

- Content, fulfilled, energized, peaceful, excited, grateful
- Frustrated, disappointed, overwhelmed, anxious, conflicted, restless

Instead of just "I like" or "I don't like," try:

- I'm drawn to, I'm curious about, I'm passionate about, I value
- I'm uncomfortable with, I'm skeptical of, I'm concerned about

Real-World Example: The Sunday Morning Ritual

Carlos and Maria developed what they called "Sunday Morning Check-ins." Every Sunday over coffee, they would ask each other three questions:

1. What's something you're excited about this week?
2. What's something you're worried or stressed about?
3. What's one way I can support you this week?

"It seems simple," Carlos explained, "but those three questions consistently led to really meaningful conversations. Sometimes we'd end up talking for two hours about things we might never have discussed otherwise."

Maria agreed: "It created a regular space for us to actually connect instead of just coordinating schedules. I felt like I got to know Carlos better and better, even after being together for several years."

Deepening Physical Intimacy Through Conversation

Real conversations create emotional intimacy, which directly impacts physical intimacy. When people feel truly known and understood, they're more likely to be vulnerable physically as well.

Conversations about desires, boundaries, fantasies, and physical connection strengthen your sexual relationship too. "What makes you feel most desired?" "What's something new you'd like to try?" "How can I help you feel more comfortable and confident?"

The Long-Term Benefits

Couples who regularly have real conversations report:

Stronger emotional connection. They feel like they truly know their partner and are known in return.

Better conflict resolution. When you understand someone's inner world, disagreements become easier to navigate.

Maintained attraction. Continuing to discover new things about your partner keeps the relationship feeling fresh and interesting.

Shared growth. Partners support each other's development because they understand each other's goals and challenges.

Greater intimacy. Emotional vulnerability creates safety for physical and spiritual intimacy.

Overcoming Resistance

"She doesn't like deep conversations." Some people haven't had positive experiences with vulnerable sharing. Create safety through consistency, acceptance, and your own appropriate vulnerability.

"I don't know what to say." Start with simple curiosity. You don't need to be a therapist; you just need to be genuinely interested.

"It feels forced." Like any skill, it might feel awkward at first. Start small and build gradually. The more you practice, the more natural it becomes.

"We don't have time." Real conversations don't require hours. Even ten minutes of genuine connection is valuable.

Advanced Conversation Skills

Reading subtext. Understanding what someone isn't saying directly but is communicating through tone, energy, or what they choose to share.

Holding space. Being comfortable with silence, emotion, and uncertainty rather than rushing to fill space or fix feelings.

Appropriate disclosure. Knowing how much to share about yourself to create connection without overwhelming or burdening.

Cultural awareness. Understanding how background and culture affect communication styles and comfort with vulnerability.

Timing sensitivity. Recognizing when someone is ready for deeper conversation versus when they need lighter interaction.

When Conversations Reveal Problems

Sometimes real conversations reveal that you and your partner have different values, goals, or expectations. This can be uncomfortable, but it's better to discover incompatibilities early rather than later.

If deep conversations reveal significant differences:

- Explore whether these are negotiable differences or deal-breakers
- Consider couples therapy to navigate major disagreements
- Appreciate the honesty that deeper communication provides
- Remember that some differences can be strengths if handled well

Key Takeaways

- Surface-level communication maintains relationships; deep conversation creates intimacy
- Real conversations require curiosity, patience, and mutual vulner-

ability
- Better questions lead to more meaningful exchanges
- Creating the right environment is crucial for deeper sharing
- Emotional vocabulary helps you navigate complex feelings and experiences
- Regular meaningful conversations keep relationships fresh and connected
- Deep conversation skills improve every relationship in your life

Action Steps

1. **Assess Your Current Conversations:** For one week, notice how much of your communication with your partner is logistical versus meaningful. What percentage involves real sharing?
2. **Implement One Deep Question Daily:** Each day, ask one question that goes beyond surface level. Start with easier topics and gradually work toward more vulnerable areas.
3. **Create a Device-Free Zone:** Designate specific times or spaces where phones and other distractions are off-limits for conversation.
4. **Practice the Three-Share Rule:** When she shares something meaningful, make three responses before changing topics: validate the feeling, ask a follow-up question, and share something related about yourself.
5. **Schedule Regular Check-ins:** Create a weekly ritual for deeper conversation, like Sunday morning coffee talks or evening walks without phones.
6. **Expand Your Emotional Vocabulary:** Learn new words for complex emotions and experiences. Notice the difference between frustrated and disappointed, between excited and content.

The goal isn't to have deep conversations 24/7. The goal is to have regular access to each other's inner worlds, to continue discovering who your partner is becoming, and to share yourself authentically.

In a world full of superficial connections, being someone who can create real intimacy through conversation is incredibly valuable. It's also one of the most reliable ways to keep long-term relationships interesting, connected, and alive.

The women in your life want to know you and be known by you. They want to share their thoughts, dreams, fears, and experiences with someone who's genuinely interested in understanding them.

That someone could be you. But only if you're willing to go beyond small talk and logistics to explore the rich inner world that every person carries with them.

6

Arguments Aren't the Enemy (Bad Arguments Are)

"We never fight."

When couples say this proudly, I often wonder what they're not talking about. Because here's the truth: healthy couples argue. They disagree, they have different perspectives, they get frustrated with each other, and they work through conflicts.

What they don't do is fight dirty, avoid all conflict, or let resentments build until they explode.

The problem isn't arguing—it's how most people argue. We learned our conflict styles from watching our parents, from movies, from trial and error. And most of us learned badly.

Dr. John Gottman's research shows that it's not whether couples fight that predicts divorce; it's how they fight. Couples who argue constructively actually have stronger, more satisfying relationships than couples who avoid conflict altogether.

The Conflict Avoidance Trap

Many people, especially those who grew up in homes with destructive conflict, develop an allergy to disagreement. They'll do almost anything to avoid arguments: agreeing when they don't actually agree, suppressing their own needs, or just hoping problems will resolve themselves.

But here's what happens when you avoid all conflict:

Problems don't get resolved, they accumulate. Small issues become big resentments over time.

You never learn how to navigate disagreement together. When conflict finally does arise, you don't have the skills to handle it constructively.

Emotional intimacy decreases. If you can't disagree safely, you can't be fully authentic with each other.

Decision-making becomes impossible. Every choice requires someone to give in rather than finding solutions that work for both people.

Resentment builds silently. The avoided conflicts don't disappear; they go underground and resurface as passive aggression, withdrawal, or contempt.

The Anatomy of Bad Arguments

Before we learn how to argue well, let's identify what makes arguments destructive:

Personal attacks. "You always..." or "You never..." or attacking character instead of addressing behavior.

Kitchen sink fighting. Bringing up every past grievance instead of focusing on the current issue.

Contempt and disrespect. Eye-rolling, name-calling, mockery, or speaking to your partner like they're stupid or worthless.

Stonewalling. Shutting down completely, giving the silent treatment, or refusing to engage.

Mind reading. "I know what you're really thinking" or assigning motives without asking.

Defensiveness. Immediately explaining why you're right instead of trying to understand their perspective.

Winning mentality. Treating arguments like battles to be won rather than problems to be solved together.

Real-World Example: The Vacation Planning Disaster

Kevin and Lisa had been together for two years, and they were planning their first big vacation together. What should have been exciting turned into a week-long fight that revealed all their worst conflict patterns.

How it started: Kevin wanted to go to Costa Rica for adventure activities. Lisa preferred Italy for culture and relaxation.

How it went wrong:

Kevin: "We always do what you want to do. You got to pick the restaurant last week, and now you want to control our vacation too."

Lisa: "That's not fair! I don't always get what I want. And since when is picking a restaurant the same as planning a whole vacation?"

Kevin: "See? You're being defensive because you know I'm right. You hate when you can't control everything."

Lisa: "I'm not controlling! I just don't want to spend our vacation sweating through jungles when we could be enjoying amazing art and food. But fine, forget I said anything. We'll do whatever you want, like always."

Kevin: "Don't do that martyr thing. If you have an opinion, just say it instead of being passive-aggressive."

Lisa: "Whatever, Kevin. You've clearly already made up your mind."

What went wrong: Personal attacks ("you always," character assassination), mind reading (assuming motives), kitchen sink fighting (bringing in past unrelated conflicts), contempt (dismissive language), and stonewalling (shutting down the conversation).

The result: They didn't go on vacation at all. The fight revealed deeper issues about decision-making, compromise, and respect that they'd never addressed.

What Good Arguments Look Like

Healthy couples don't avoid conflict—they engage with it skillfully. Here's what constructive arguments include:

Focus on specific behaviors, not character. "I felt hurt when you made plans without checking with me" instead of "You're so inconsiderate."

Use "I" statements. Express your feelings and needs rather than attacking or blaming.

Stay on topic. Address the current issue without bringing in past grievances or unrelated problems.

Listen to understand. Try to genuinely understand your partner's perspective before defending your own.

Look for solutions together. Treat the problem as something you're solving together, not a battle you're fighting against each other.

Take breaks when needed. If emotions get too high, pause the conversation and return when you can engage constructively.

Repair attempts. Use humor, affection, or acknowledgment to de-escalate tension during the conversation.

The Costa Rica/Italy Conversation, Done Right

Here's how Kevin and Lisa could have handled their vacation disagreement constructively:

Kevin: "I'm really excited about this vacation, and I've been looking forward to doing some adventure activities. I know you mentioned Italy—help me understand what appeals to you about that."

Lisa: "I've been feeling really stressed with work lately, and I was imagining something more relaxing. Plus, I've always wanted to see the art in Florence. What kind of adventure stuff were you thinking about in Costa Rica?"

Kevin: "Hiking, maybe some zip-lining, seeing wildlife. I spend so much time at a desk that I'm craving something active. But I hear you about needing relaxation. What if we looked for a place that could give us both?"

Lisa: "That's a good idea. Or maybe we could do a shorter trip somewhere active and plan a more relaxing long weekend another time?"

Kevin: "I like that. What feels most important to you for this particular vacation?"

What made this better: They stayed curious about each other's needs, looked for solutions together, and treated it as a problem to solve rather than a battle to win.

The Pre-Argument Skills

The most important conflict resolution happens before the argument starts:

Build a foundation of respect. When you genuinely respect your partner, you're less likely to attack their character during disagreements.

Address small issues early. Don't let minor irritations build into major resentments.

Understand your triggers. Know what topics or behaviors tend to escalate your emotions, and prepare strategies for staying calm.

Practice emotional regulation. Develop tools for managing your emotional reactions during conflict.

Create agreements about how you'll disagree. Discuss your conflict styles and agree on ground rules when you're not in the middle of an argument.

During the Argument: The STOP Method

When you find yourself in a heated discussion, use this framework:

S - Stop and breathe. Take a moment to regulate your emotions before responding.

T - Think about their perspective. Try to understand why they feel the way they do.

O - Own your part. Acknowledge how you've contributed to the problem or misunderstanding.

P - Problem-solve together. Focus on finding solutions rather than proving who's right.

Common Argument Patterns and How to Break Them

The Escalation Spiral

One person gets louder, the other gets louder, until you're both yelling about things that have nothing to do with the original issue.

Break it: Lower your voice. Often, the other person will match your volume. If things are getting too heated, call for a time-out.

The Withdraw-Pursue Cycle

One person wants to talk things through immediately; the other needs space to process. The pursuer feels abandoned; the withdrawer feels overwhelmed.

Break it: Agree on when you'll return to the conversation. "I need 30 minutes to think about this, then let's talk."

The Blame Game

Each person focuses on what the other did wrong instead of taking responsibility for their own actions.

Break it: Start with your own accountability. "I realize I contributed to this by..."

The History Lesson

Bringing up everything that's ever gone wrong instead of focusing on the current issue.

Break it: "Let's focus on what's happening now. We can talk about those other things later if we need to."

The Art of Repair

Even good arguers make mistakes during conflict. The key is learning to repair the damage quickly:

Acknowledge when you've been unfair. "I'm sorry, that was harsh. Let me try again."

Use humor appropriately. Sometimes a well-timed joke can defuse tension (but never at your partner's expense).

Take responsibility for your emotions. "I'm getting defensive, which isn't helpful. Give me a second."

Refocus on connection. "I love you, and I want us to figure this out together."

Physical affection. Sometimes a gentle touch can remind you both that you're on the same team.

Real-World Example: Mark and Sarah's Transformation

Mark and Sarah used to have explosive fights that would last for days and leave them both feeling awful. Their pattern was predictable: one would raise a concern, the other would get defensive, voices would escalate, past grievances would get dragged in, and eventually someone would storm out.

The turning point came after a particularly bad fight about household responsibilities that ended with Sarah sleeping on the couch for three nights.

"We realized that our way of arguing was actually damaging our relationship," Mark explained. "We weren't solving anything; we were just hurting each other."

They developed what they called "argument rules":

1. No personal attacks or character assassination
2. Stay on the current topic
3. Take a break if emotions get too high
4. Both people have to take responsibility for their part
5. The goal is understanding and solutions, not winning

"It felt artificial at first," Sarah admitted. "But after a few months, we realized our conflicts were actually bringing us closer together instead of driving us apart. We were solving problems instead of just venting frustration."

The Time-Out Strategy

Sometimes emotions run too high for productive conversation. Here's how to take a break without it feeling like abandonment:

Call it early. Don't wait until you're both screaming. "I'm getting too emotional to have this conversation well right now."

Set a return time. "Let's take 20 minutes and then try again." This prevents it from becoming avoidance.

Use the time productively. Cool down, think about the other person's perspective, consider your own contribution to the problem.

Return as promised. Don't use time-outs as a way to avoid difficult conversations altogether.

Arguments About Arguments

Sometimes you need to have meta-conversations about how you're communicating:

"I noticed we both got really defensive in that conversation. How can we approach this differently?"

"I feel like we keep having the same argument over and over. What are we missing?"

"When you raise your voice, I shut down. Can we try a different approach?"

The Apology Framework

Good apologies have four components:

Acknowledgment: "I was wrong to interrupt you repeatedly during that conversation."

Responsibility: "I was feeling defensive, but that's not an excuse for not listening to you."

Empathy: "I imagine that felt frustrating and disrespectful."

Action: "I'm going to work on managing my defensiveness better, and I want to hear what you were trying to tell me."

Fighting Fair Ground Rules

Establish these agreements when you're not in conflict:

No name-calling or personal attacks

No bringing up past issues unless they're directly relevant

No threats about the relationship ("Maybe we should just break up")

Take breaks when emotions get too high

No attacking someone's family or friends

Focus on behavior, not character

Both people get to express their perspective

The goal is understanding and solutions, not winning

When Arguments Reveal Deeper Issues

Sometimes surface disagreements point to underlying problems:

The dishwasher argument might really be about feeling unappreciated or carrying unequal household responsibility.

The money argument might be about different values, security fears, or power dynamics.

The social plans argument might be about introversion vs. extraversion or different social needs.

When the same arguments keep recurring, look for the deeper issue underneath the surface complaint.

The Benefits of Good Arguments

Couples who argue constructively experience:

Better problem-solving. They actually resolve issues instead of just venting about them.

Increased intimacy. Working through conflict together builds trust and connection.

Better understanding. They learn about each other's needs, fears, and perspectives.

Improved communication skills. They get better at expressing themselves and listening to each other.

Stronger relationships. They know they can navigate difficulties together.

Red Flags in Arguments

Some argument behaviors are serious warning signs:

Physical intimidation or violence

Threats or ultimatums designed to control

Cruel personal attacks designed to wound

Consistent contempt or disgust

Complete refusal to engage or work on issues

Bringing in third parties to gang up on your partner

Using someone's vulnerabilities against them

If these patterns are present, professional help is essential.

Advanced Conflict Resolution Skills

Emotional validation during disagreement. "I can see why you'd feel that way, even though I see it differently."

Finding the kernel of truth. Looking for what's valid in your partner's perspective, even when you disagree with most of it.

Collaborative problem-solving. "What would a solution look like that addresses both of our concerns?"

Repair and reconnection. Rebuilding intimacy after conflict through affection, appreciation, or shared activities.

The Long-Term View

Remember that the goal isn't to eliminate all disagreement from your relationship. The goal is to disagree in ways that strengthen your connection rather than damage it.

Every couple will face conflicts about money, sex, family, career decisions, household responsibilities, and life direction. The couples who thrive are the ones who learn to navigate these inevitable disagreements with respect, curiosity, and commitment to finding solutions together.

Key Takeaways

- Healthy couples argue; unhealthy couples either fight destructively or avoid conflict entirely
- Good arguments focus on specific issues, use respectful language, and aim for solutions
- Personal attacks, contempt, and stonewalling are relationship killers
- Time-outs can prevent arguments from becoming destructive
- Repair attempts during and after arguments are crucial for maintaining connection
- Many surface arguments reflect deeper underlying issues
- Learning to argue well strengthens relationships rather than damaging them

Action Steps

1. **Identify Your Conflict Style:** Reflect on how you typically handle disagreements. Do you attack, defend, withdraw, or problem-solve? What patterns have you learned from your family of origin?

2. **Establish Ground Rules:** Have a conversation with your partner about how you want to handle disagreements. Create agreements about what's fair and what's off-limits.

3. **Practice the STOP Method:** Next time you feel a conflict escalating, try: Stop and breathe, Think about their perspective, Own your part, Problem-solve together.

4. **Learn Your Triggers:** Notice what topics or behaviors consistently escalate your emotions. Develop strategies for staying calm when these triggers arise.

5. **Try the 24-Hour Rule:** For non-urgent conflicts, wait 24 hours before bringing up your concern. This helps you approach the issue more thoughtfully.

6. **Focus on One Issue at a Time:** In your next disagreement, consciously avoid bringing up past problems or unrelated issues. Stay focused on the current concern.

Arguments are inevitable in any close relationship. The question isn't whether you'll disagree with your partner—it's whether you'll disagree in ways that bring you closer together or drive you apart.

Learning to argue well is one of the most valuable relationship skills you can develop. It shows your partner that you can handle conflict without attacking them personally, that you're committed to working through problems together, and that your relationship is safe for authentic expression.

The women in your life don't need you to agree with them about everything. But they do need to know that when you disagree, you'll do it with respect, that you'll listen to their perspective, and that you're committed to finding solutions that work for both of you.

That's not just good arguing—that's good partnership.

III

Respect and Partnership

7

Respect Isn't Just Holding Doors Open

"He says he respects women, but then he interrupts me constantly and dismisses my opinions when they differ from his."

This observation from Claire captures one of the most common relationship blind spots: the gap between surface-level courtesy and genuine respect.

Many men were raised to show traditional forms of politeness toward women—opening doors, paying for dinner, helping with coats. These gestures can be lovely, but they're not the same as true respect. In fact, some men use these surface behaviors to convince themselves (and others) that they're respectful while engaging in patterns that are actually quite disrespectful.

Real respect in modern relationships goes much deeper than social courtesies. It's about seeing your partner as a complete, capable, intelligent person whose thoughts, feelings, and autonomy deserve the same consideration you'd want for yourself.

What Respect Actually Looks Like

Respect isn't just about being polite or avoiding obviously offensive behavior. It's about how you treat someone when you disagree with them, when you're frustrated, when they're not performing the way you want, and when no one else is watching.

Respect is believing she's competent. This means not explaining things she already knows, not second-guessing her decisions in her areas of expertise, and not treating her like she needs your permission to make choices about her own life.

Respect is valuing her perspective. Even when you disagree, you recognize that her viewpoint comes from her experiences and intelligence, not from confusion or emotion.

Respect is honoring her autonomy. She gets to make her own decisions about her career, her body, her friendships, and her life, even when you might choose differently.

Respect is treating her as an equal. Not as someone you need to protect, manage, or improve, but as a partner whose judgment and capabilities you trust.

The Subtle Forms of Disrespect

Many disrespectful behaviors are so normalized that people don't recognize them as problematic:

Mansplaining: Explaining things she already knows or understands, often in areas where she has more expertise than you do.

Interrupting consistently: Cutting her off mid-sentence, especially when she's expressing opinions or sharing experiences.

Dismissive body language: Eye-rolling, checking your phone while she talks, or sighing when she brings up concerns.

Making decisions for her: Ordering her food, speaking for her in social situations, or making plans that affect her without asking.

Questioning her emotions: "Are you sure you're not overreacting?" "Is this about your period?" "You're being too sensitive."

Minimizing her accomplishments: Attributing her success to luck, connections, or anything other than her competence and hard work.

The selective listener: Tuning in when she's talking about things that interest you but zoning out when she discusses her work, interests, or concerns.

Real-World Example: The Expert in the Room

Jessica is a financial advisor with ten years of experience and multiple certifications. Her boyfriend Ryan works in marketing and has no formal financial training.

At a dinner party, the conversation turned to investing. When Jessica started sharing insights about market trends, Ryan interrupted her multiple times to "correct" her information—information that was actually accurate and based on her professional expertise.

Later, when another guest asked about retirement planning, Ryan answered for Jessica, getting several important details wrong while she sat silently, increasingly frustrated.

"It was so embarrassing," Jessica told me later. "Not just because he was wrong about things that are literally my job, but because he automatically assumed he knew better than I did. It felt like he doesn't actually see me as competent, despite all my training and experience."

When Jessica brought this up with Ryan later, his response was defensive: "I was just trying to be part of the conversation. I respect you."

But respect isn't something you claim to have—it's something you demonstrate through your actions.

The Competence Assumption

One of the most important aspects of respect is assuming your partner is competent unless proven otherwise, rather than assuming incompetence until proven otherwise.

This means:

- If she's handling something, assume she can handle it well
- If she makes a decision you wouldn't make, assume she has good reasons
- If she's struggling with something, offer support rather than taking over
- If she has expertise in an area, defer to her knowledge

This doesn't mean:

- Never offering help or input
- Agreeing with everything she says
- Pretending she never makes mistakes
- Avoiding collaboration or shared decision-making

The difference is in your default assumption: competent partner who might occasionally need support, or incompetent person who needs constant guidance.

Respect During Disagreement

It's easy to be respectful when you agree with someone. The real test comes during conflicts and disagreements.

Respectful disagreement includes:

- Listening to understand her perspective before arguing your point
- Acknowledging what's valid in her position, even if you disagree overall
- Focusing on the specific issue rather than attacking her character or judgment
- Speaking to her the way you'd want to be spoken to during conflict
- Recognizing that two intelligent people can look at the same situation and reach different conclusions

Disrespectful disagreement includes:

- Dismissing her concerns as "emotional" or "irrational"
- Using her past mistakes to discredit her current point
- Raising your voice or using intimidating body language
- Making her wrong about everything rather than finding areas of agreement
- Treating disagreement as a battle to be won rather than a problem to be solved together

The Autonomy Question

Respect means recognizing that your partner is the ultimate authority on her own life. This can be challenging for men who were raised to see themselves as protectors or leaders in relationships.

She gets to decide:

- What career path to pursue
- How to spend her free time
- What relationships to maintain
- How to handle conflicts with her family
- What she wears and how she presents herself

- Whether and when to have children
- How to manage her health and body

Your role is to:

- Support her decisions, even when you might choose differently
- Offer your perspective when asked
- Express concerns respectfully if her choices affect you directly
- Be a sounding board when she's working through difficult decisions

This doesn't mean you can't have preferences or that her choices never affect you. It means recognizing that she's capable of making good decisions for herself, and that those decisions are ultimately hers to make.

Respect in Daily Interactions

Respect shows up in countless small moments throughout everyday life:

In conversation:

- Giving her your full attention when she's speaking
- Asking follow-up questions about things that matter to her
- Remembering important details from previous conversations
- Sharing airtime rather than dominating discussions

In social situations:

- Not speaking for her unless she's asked you to
- Including her in conversations rather than talking around her

- Backing up her statements when she's correct
- Not undermining her in front of others, even jokingly

In decision-making:

- Consulting her about decisions that affect both of you
- Valuing her input on important choices
- Not presenting her with fait accompli when collaboration was expected
- Recognizing her expertise in areas where she knows more than you do

The Emotional Respect Gap

Many men struggle with respecting women's emotional experiences, often because they've been taught that emotions are less valid than logic.

Emotional respect means:

- Believing her emotions are real and valid, even if you don't understand them
- Recognizing that emotions contain information, not just noise
- Understanding that "rational" and "emotional" aren't opposites— good decisions often require both
- Supporting her through difficult emotions rather than trying to fix or eliminate them

Common emotional disrespect:

- "You're overreacting"
- "Don't be so emotional"

- "That doesn't make sense"
- "Just calm down"
- "You're being irrational"

Real-World Example: The Career Decision

When Amanda got offered a promotion that would require relocating to another city, her husband Mike's first reaction was to start listing all the reasons why it was a bad idea: they'd be farther from family, their house would be hard to sell, his job was going well where they were.

Amanda felt like Mike was trying to make the decision for her rather than supporting her through a difficult choice.

The conversation changed when Mike shifted his approach: "This sounds like an amazing opportunity, and also like a complex decision with a lot of factors to consider. How are you feeling about it? What would help you think through all the implications?"

Instead of immediately advocating for his preferred outcome, Mike respected Amanda's right to make this decision and offered to support her decision-making process.

"It made such a difference," Amanda explained later. "I needed to process all the implications myself, and I needed to know that whatever I decided, Mike would be supportive rather than resentful."

Professional Respect

Many relationship respect issues emerge around career and professional life:

Respecting her career means:

- Understanding that her work matters as much as yours
- Not expecting her to sacrifice career opportunities for your conve-

nience
- Sharing household responsibilities rather than assuming her career is secondary
- Supporting her professional relationships and networking
- Celebrating her successes without trying to diminish them
- Not using her income or professional status to measure her worth

Career disrespect includes:

- Referring to her job as "her little career" or similar diminishing language
- Assuming she'll handle all child care or household management because "her job is more flexible"
- Expecting her to move for your career without reciprocal consideration
- Not taking her work problems seriously
- Making jokes about her profession or colleagues

Intellectual Respect

This is about recognizing that she's as intelligent and capable of complex thinking as you are, even if she thinks differently or has different areas of expertise.

Intellectual respect includes:

- Engaging seriously with her ideas and opinions
- Not automatically assuming you know more about topics she's discussing
- Asking genuine questions about her thoughts rather than leading questions designed to prove your point
- Acknowledging when she makes good points or changes your

perspective
- Learning from her expertise and experience

The Respect-Attraction Connection

Here's something many men don't realize: respect is incredibly attractive. When you genuinely respect someone, it shows in how you interact with them, and that creates a positive dynamic that strengthens the relationship.

Respect creates attraction because:

- It makes her feel valued and appreciated for who she really is
- It creates emotional safety, which allows for vulnerability and intimacy
- It demonstrates that you see her as an equal, which is the foundation of healthy partnership
- It shows confidence in yourself—secure people can respect others without feeling threatened

When Respect Is Challenged

Sometimes respecting your partner means supporting decisions you wouldn't make or opinions you don't share. This can be challenging, but it's essential for healthy relationships.

Guidelines for difficult situations:

- You can disagree with her choices while still respecting her right to make them
- Express concerns honestly but without trying to control the outcome
- Focus on being supportive rather than being right

- Remember that she doesn't need to make the same choices you would make
- Trust that she knows herself and her situation better than you do

Building a Culture of Mutual Respect

Create agreements about respect: Discuss what respect means to both of you and how you want to treat each other.

Call out disrespect gently: When you notice yourself being disrespectful, acknowledge it and correct course.

Model the respect you want: Treat her with the same respect you'd want in return.

Make respect non-negotiable: Some behaviors should be automatic deal-breakers in healthy relationships.

Celebrate competence: Notice and acknowledge her skills, insights, and successes.

Respect Across Different Areas

Financial respect: Including her in money decisions, not controlling her spending unreasonably, recognizing her financial contributions whether they're monetary or otherwise.

Sexual respect: Recognizing her autonomy over her own body, communicating about desires and boundaries, never pressuring or coercing.

Social respect: Not embarrassing her in front of others, supporting her friendships, treating her family with courtesy.

Physical respect: Respecting her space, not using physical intimidation during arguments, asking before touching in ways that might be unwelcome.

The Long-Term Benefits

Relationships built on genuine respect are:

More satisfying for both people: When you feel respected, you feel valued and appreciated.

More stable: Respect creates a foundation of trust and safety that helps relationships weather difficulties.

More intimate: When someone feels respected, they're more likely to be vulnerable and open.

More collaborative: Respected partners work together more effectively as a team.

More attractive: Respect creates positive dynamics that maintain attraction over time.

Common Respect Mistakes

The helper complex: Constantly trying to rescue or improve her instead of trusting her competence.

The advisor: Always offering unsolicited advice instead of just listening and supporting.

The manager: Trying to organize her life or make decisions for her.

The critic: Constantly pointing out what she's doing wrong or how she could do better.

The competitor: Turning everything into a contest instead of celebrating her successes.

When You've Been Disrespectful

Acknowledge it quickly: "I realized I was being dismissive just now, and I'm sorry."

Take responsibility: Don't make excuses or blame your behavior on stress, tiredness, or other factors.

Make concrete changes: Show through your actions that you're committed to being more respectful.

Ask how to do better: "How can I show you more respect in situations like this?"

Key Takeaways

- Real respect goes far beyond surface politeness to genuine recognition of your partner's competence and autonomy
- Many forms of disrespect are so normalized that people don't recognize them as problematic
- Respect during disagreement is the true test of how you value your partner
- Assuming competence rather than incompetence is fundamental to respectful relationships
- Emotional experiences deserve as much respect as logical arguments
- Professional and intellectual respect are crucial components of modern relationships
- Respect and attraction are closely connected—respect creates the conditions for lasting attraction

Action Steps

1. **Assess Your Respect Patterns:** For one week, notice how you interact with your partner during disagreements, decision-making, and daily conversations. Are you demonstrating respect or falling into dismissive patterns?
2. **Practice the Competence Assumption:** Next time your partner is handling something, resist the urge to offer unsolicited advice

or take over. Assume she's got it handled unless she specifically asks for help.

3. **Check Your Interrupting:** Pay attention to whether you interrupt her during conversations. If you catch yourself doing it, apologize and ask her to continue.

4. **Validate During Disagreement:** In your next disagreement, practice acknowledging what's valid in her perspective before presenting your own viewpoint.

5. **Support Her Expertise:** Identify areas where she has more knowledge or experience than you do, and practice deferring to her judgment in those areas.

6. **Have the Respect Conversation:** Talk with your partner about what respect means to each of you and how you can better demonstrate it in your relationship.

Respect isn't something you show only to people you agree with or people who are behaving the way you want them to behave. Real respect is a consistent way of treating someone because you recognize their inherent worth and competence as a person.

The women in your life don't need you to put them on a pedestal or treat them like fragile flowers who need protection. They need you to treat them like the capable, intelligent, autonomous individuals they are.

That's not just respectful—it's the foundation of genuine partnership.

8

The Mental Load Revolution

"I don't mind doing the dishes. What I mind is being the only one who remembers that we need dish soap, that the sponges are getting gross, and that we're almost out of clean towels. I mind being the household CEO while he gets to be the helpful employee who does tasks when asked."

This comment from Rachel captures one of the most invisible yet relationship-damaging dynamics in modern partnerships: the mental load imbalance.

The mental load is the invisible work of keeping track of everything that needs to be done, when it needs to happen, and who's responsible for it. It's remembering that your nephew has a birthday next week, noticing when you're running low on groceries, keeping track of everyone's schedules, and managing the thousand small details that keep a household and relationship functioning.

In many relationships, women carry a disproportionate share of this invisible labor, and it's exhausting them.

What the Mental Load Actually Is

The mental load isn't just about remembering to buy milk. It's about being the person who:

Keeps the master calendar - Knowing everyone's schedules, appointments, and commitments

Manages social relationships - Remembering birthdays, planning social activities, maintaining friendships for both of you

Monitors household needs - Noticing when things are running low, need replacing, or aren't working properly

Plans for the future - Thinking ahead about meals, events, seasonal changes, and long-term needs

Handles emotional labor - Managing family relationships, mediating conflicts, remembering what's important to people

Coordinates logistics - Planning trips, managing multiple calendars, ensuring everyone gets where they need to go

This mental work is happening constantly, running in the background of someone's mind like an operating system that never shuts down.

The Invisible Nature of Mental Labor

One reason mental load imbalances persist is that this work is largely invisible. When someone does laundry, you can see the clean clothes. When someone takes out trash, the bin is empty. But when someone spends mental energy keeping track of what needs to happen, there's no visible product.

You can't see:

· The mental energy spent remembering your mother's birthday and buying a card

- The cognitive work of meal planning for the week
- The emotional labor of noticing your partner seems stressed and checking in
- The scheduling juggle of coordinating everyone's activities
- The anticipatory work of thinking about what might be needed for upcoming events

You can see:

- The birthday card that arrives on time
- The dinner that appears on the table
- The conflict that gets resolved
- The smooth coordination of activities
- The preparedness for events

This invisibility means that the person carrying the mental load often doesn't get credit for this work, while the person not carrying it may not even realize how much is being managed.

Real-World Example: The Birthday Party Planning

When their daughter's seventh birthday approached, Monica automatically started the mental planning process: guest list, theme, decorations, cake, activities, party favors, invitations, cleanup plan. She was thinking about weather backup plans, dietary restrictions, and how to make sure no one felt left out.

Her husband Alex was happy to help when asked. He could pick up decorations, set up tables, or handle cleanup. But he never initiated any of the planning or thinking ahead.

"The party was successful," Monica explained, "but I was exhausted. Not because of the physical work—we shared that pretty equally. I was exhausted from being the only one carrying all the mental work of thinking through every detail and coordinating everything."

From Alex's perspective, he was being helpful and involved. He'd contributed equally to the physical tasks. What he didn't realize was that Monica had been working on this party in her head for weeks before he ever had to think about it.

The "Just Tell Me What to Do" Problem

Many well-meaning partners try to address imbalances by saying, "Just tell me what needs to be done, and I'll do it." This seems helpful, but it actually maintains the mental load imbalance.

When you say "just tell me what to do," you're essentially saying: "I'll be the employee, but you have to be the manager. You figure out what needs to happen, when, and how, and then delegate tasks to me."

This means your partner is still:

- Keeping track of everything that needs to be done
- Prioritizing tasks and timing
- Breaking big projects into manageable steps
- Following up to make sure things get completed
- Managing the emotional labor of asking for help repeatedly

The Manager vs. Partner Dynamic

The manager (often the woman) is responsible for:

- Seeing what needs to be done
- Planning how and when to do it
- Delegating tasks to others
- Following up on completion

- Handling the emotional work of coordination
- Being the "bad guy" who has to ask for help

The employee (often the man) is responsible for:

- Completing assigned tasks
- Doing what's asked when it's asked
- Being helpful and cooperative

The problem is that romantic partnerships should be between two managers, not a manager and an employee. Both people should be equally invested in noticing what needs to happen and taking initiative to make it happen.

Why This Pattern Develops

Socialization differences: Many women were raised to notice and manage domestic and emotional needs, while many men were taught that these things would be handled by someone else.

Different standards: Research shows that women and men often have different thresholds for cleanliness, organization, and social maintenance. When your standard is lower, you literally don't see the need for action until later.

The competence trap: If one person is better at organizing or planning, it becomes easy for them to take over these responsibilities entirely.

The gratitude dynamic: When mental load carriers get appreciation for managing everything well, it can reinforce the pattern rather than changing it.

Time availability assumptions: If one person has a more flexible schedule, they often end up carrying more mental load by default.

The Emotional Cost

Carrying a disproportionate mental load has significant emotional consequences:

Mental exhaustion: The cognitive work of keeping track of everything is genuinely tiring.

Resentment: Feeling like you're the only one who cares about things getting done creates anger and frustration.

Feeling unappreciated: The invisible nature of mental work means it often goes unrecognized.

Loss of spontaneity: When you're always thinking ahead and planning, it's hard to be present and spontaneous.

Relationship inequality: The dynamic starts feeling more parental than partnership-based.

Reduced intimacy: It's hard to feel romantic toward someone you feel like you have to manage.

Real-World Example: The Vacation That Wasn't Relaxing

Ben and Sophia went on what was supposed to be a relaxing beach vacation. Ben was excited to finally unwind and not think about anything. Sophia spent the vacation:

- Making sure they had sunscreen and that it got reapplied
- Planning meals and coordinating restaurant reservations
- Keeping track of everyone's belongings and activities
- Managing social interactions with other couples they met
- Thinking ahead about packing for the flight home
- Handling the emotional work when their teenage son got moody

"Ben had a great, relaxing vacation," Sophia said afterward. "I felt like

I was working the whole time, just in a different location. He got to be completely present and spontaneous because I was handling all the mental work of keeping everything organized."

The Mental Load Audit

To understand your mental load distribution, try this exercise. List all the ongoing responsibilities in your relationship and household:

Household Management:

- Meal planning and grocery shopping awareness
- Cleaning schedules and standards maintenance
- Laundry systems and clothing care
- Home maintenance and repair coordination
- Financial management and bill tracking
- Seasonal preparation (winterizing, spring cleaning)

Social and Emotional Labor:

- Maintaining relationships with both families
- Remembering birthdays and special occasions
- Planning social activities and date nights
- Managing conflicts and emotional check-ins
- Holiday planning and gift coordination
- Community involvement and social obligations

Logistics and Planning:

- Calendar coordination and scheduling
- Travel planning and preparation
- Healthcare appointments and follow-up

- Children's activities and school involvement
- Pet care coordination
- Long-term goal planning

Now ask: Who currently carries the mental responsibility for noticing, planning, and coordinating each area?**

Becoming a Mental Load Partner

The goal isn't to split everything 50/50 down the middle. It's for both people to function as equal partners who are both invested in noticing what needs to happen and taking initiative to make it happen.

Develop systems awareness: Start noticing the systems that keep your life running. What needs to happen for your household to function well? Who's currently managing these systems?

Practice proactive thinking: Instead of waiting to be told what to do, start anticipating needs. Look ahead at the calendar. Notice when things are running low. Think about what might be needed for upcoming events.

Take ownership of specific areas: Rather than just helping with everything, become the primary person responsible for certain domains. Own them completely, including the planning and mental work.

Communicate about invisible work: Make the mental labor visible by talking about it. "I've been thinking about your mom's visit next month. Should we plan some activities, or does she prefer just hanging out?"

Creating Shared Mental Responsibility

Weekly planning meetings: Spend 15 minutes each week looking at the upcoming week together. What needs to happen? Who's handling what? What potential challenges do you see?

Monthly big picture check-ins: Look ahead at the coming month. What events, appointments, or deadlines are approaching? What planning needs to happen?

Seasonal transitions: Take turns being the person who thinks ahead about seasonal changes, holiday planning, or major transitions.

Project ownership: For big projects (renovations, vacations, parties), have one person be the primary project manager, but alternate who takes this role.

Emergency preparedness: Both people should know where important documents are, have access to accounts, and understand key household systems.

The Art of Noticing

Mental load partnership requires developing better situational awareness:

Practice environmental scanning: Regularly look around and notice what needs attention. Are we low on household supplies? Do any household items need maintenance or replacement?

Develop calendar consciousness: Be aware of what's coming up, not just for you but for the household/family unit.

Tune into emotional climates: Notice when your partner seems stressed, tired, or overwhelmed, and check in proactively.

Think systems, not just tasks: Instead of just doing dishes, think about the whole kitchen system. Do we have enough dish soap? Are the sponges getting gross? Is the dishwasher working properly?

Real-World Example: Jake's Mental Load Awakening

Daniel realized he had a mental load problem when his wife Natalie made a comment about feeling like his "executive assistant." Initially defensive, Daniel started paying attention to their division of mental labor.

What he discovered was eye-opening: Natalie was keeping track of their social calendar, managing relationships with both sets of parents, remembering important dates, planning meals, monitoring household supplies, and coordinating their schedules, while Daniel was primarily responsible for taking out trash and mowing the lawn.

Daniel's transformation involved taking complete ownership of several areas:

- **Meal planning:** He took over planning meals for the week, creating grocery lists, and ensuring they had ingredients for planned meals.
- **Social calendar:** He became the primary person coordinating their social activities and maintaining friendships.
- **Home maintenance:** He developed systems for tracking when things needed attention and scheduling repairs or maintenance.
- **Gift and event coordination:** He took over remembering birthdays and planning celebrations.

"The crazy thing," Daniel said, "was how much mental energy Natalie had been using that I didn't even notice. When I started carrying some of that load, I realized how much work it really is to keep everything organized and running smoothly."

Common Mental Load Mistakes

The grand gesture fallacy: Thinking that occasionally planning something big compensates for not handling ongoing mental work.

The helper mentality: Continuing to see yourself as someone who helps rather than someone who's equally responsible for noticing and planning.

The expertise excuse: "She's better at planning" becomes a reason to avoid developing your own planning and organizational skills.

The different standards dodge: Using different cleanliness or organization standards as an excuse not to participate in maintaining household systems.

The busy schedule rationalization: Assuming that whoever has more flexibility should automatically carry more mental load.

The Technology Solution

Modern tools can help distribute mental load more equally:

Shared calendars: Both people can see and add to family schedules

Shared task lists: Apps like Todoist or Any.do that both partners can access and update

Automated reminders: Set up systems that remind both people about recurring tasks

Shared grocery lists: Apps that both people can add to throughout the week

Photo sharing: Document things that need attention so both people can see them

The key is that both people need to actively use these systems, not just have access to them.

When Mental Load Becomes Overwhelming

Sometimes mental load imbalances become so severe that they require more intensive intervention:

Signs of mental load overwhelm:

- Constant feeling of mental exhaustion
- Resentment about being the only one who "cares" about things getting done
- Feeling like you can never fully relax because you're always thinking about what needs to happen
- Anxiety about things falling through the cracks
- Feeling more like a household manager than a romantic partner

Intervention strategies:

- Take a complete break from certain responsibilities while your partner takes them over entirely
- Seek couples therapy to address the pattern and learn new ways of sharing responsibility
- Have intensive conversations about values and priorities to align on what actually needs to be managed
- Consider outside help (cleaning service, meal delivery, professional organizers) to reduce the overall load

The Long-Term Benefits

When mental load is shared more equally:

Both people feel more supported: Neither person feels like they're carrying everything alone.

Relationships feel more equal: The parent-child dynamic disappears when both people are equally invested in managing life together.

Stress levels decrease: When responsibility is shared, neither person feels overwhelmed by the coordination work.

Intimacy improves: It's easier to feel romantic toward someone who's your partner rather than someone you have to manage.

Both people develop skills: Everyone becomes more capable and self-sufficient.

Flexibility increases: If one person is unavailable, the other can handle coordination without everything falling apart.

Advanced Mental Load Sharing

Anticipatory teamwork: Both people thinking ahead and communicating about potential needs or challenges.

System optimization: Working together to create efficient systems that reduce the overall mental load for both people.

Emotional labor balance: Sharing not just logistical coordination but also the work of maintaining relationships and managing family dynamics.

Crisis management: Both people prepared to handle emergencies or unexpected situations without falling back into old patterns.

Key Takeaways

- Mental load is the invisible work of keeping track of everything that needs to happen in a household and relationship
- "Just tell me what to do" maintains the imbalance by keeping one person in the manager role
- Mental load imbalances create resentment, exhaustion, and relationship inequality
- True partnership means both people taking initiative to notice what

needs attention

- Sharing mental load requires developing systems awareness and proactive thinking
- Technology can help, but both people need to actively participate in shared systems
- Equal mental load distribution strengthens relationships and reduces stress for both partners

Action Steps

1. **Complete a Mental Load Audit:** List all the ongoing responsibilities in your relationship and honestly assess who currently carries the mental responsibility for each area.
2. **Take Complete Ownership of Three Areas:** Choose three domains where you'll become the primary person responsible for both the doing and the thinking/planning.
3. **Develop Weekly Planning Habits:** Implement a 15-minute weekly check-in where you both look at the upcoming week and coordinate responsibilities.
4. **Practice Proactive Noticing:** For one week, actively scan your environment and relationship for things that need attention, rather than waiting to be told.
5. **Have the Mental Load Conversation:** Discuss this concept with your partner. What mental load is she currently carrying that she'd like to share? What systems could you implement to distribute responsibility more evenly?
6. **Use Technology Strategically:** Implement one shared digital system (calendar, task list, or grocery list) that both of you actively use.

The mental load revolution isn't about doing more tasks—it's about thinking like a partner rather than an employee. It's about being equally invested in noticing what needs attention and taking initiative to handle it.

When both people in a relationship function as partners rather than manager and employee, it creates a dynamic of mutual support and shared responsibility that strengthens the relationship and reduces stress for both people.

The women in your life don't need you to do everything. They need you to notice everything, think ahead about what might be needed, and take initiative to handle things without being asked.

That's not just helpful—it's true partnership.

9

Supporting Her Dreams (Even When They're Bigger Than Yours)

"I want to support her, but her dreams scare me."

This honest admission from Tyler captures one of the most challenging aspects of modern relationships: what happens when your partner's ambitions are larger, different from, or potentially threatening to your own goals and comfort zone.

Maybe she wants to start her own business while you prefer the security of steady employment. Maybe she's considering going back to school for a degree that would require significant time and financial investment. Maybe she's passionate about a career path that would require relocating, traveling frequently, or earning significantly more than you do.

Here's the uncomfortable truth: many relationships don't survive when one partner outgrows the other or pursues dreams that challenge the established dynamic. But the healthiest, most satisfying relationships are built between two people who actively support each other's growth and success, even when it's scary or inconvenient.

The Growth vs. Security Dilemma

Most people want both growth and security, but these desires often conflict. Supporting your partner's biggest dreams sometimes means accepting uncertainty, change, and challenges to your established way of life.

Security-focused thinking says:

- "What if she becomes too successful and doesn't need me anymore?"
- "What if pursuing this dream puts financial strain on us?"
- "What if she changes and we grow apart?"
- "What if this affects our current lifestyle negatively?"

Growth-focused thinking says:

- "How can I help her achieve something that's important to her?"
- "What would it mean for our relationship if she felt supported in pursuing her dreams?"
- "How can we navigate the challenges together?"
- "What opportunities might this create for both of us?"

Both perspectives are understandable, but only one builds strong, lasting relationships.

Real-World Example: The MBA Dilemma

When Vanessa told her boyfriend Craig that she wanted to pursue an MBA at a prestigious program three hours away, his first reaction was panic disguised as practicality.

"How are we going to see each other?" Craig asked. "What about your job here? And MBA programs are expensive—is it really worth the debt?"

What Craig didn't say, but was really thinking: *What if she meets someone more ambitious than me? What if she decides I'm not successful enough for her new life? What if she realizes she can do better?*

Vanessa felt Craig's resistance and started downplaying her excitement about the program. "Maybe it's not the right time," she said. "Maybe I should wait a few years."

But the damage was already done. Vanessa began to see Craig as someone who would hold her back rather than support her growth. The relationship ended six months later, not because of the MBA program, but because Vanessa realized she needed a partner who would celebrate her ambitions rather than fear them.

Why Supporting Dreams Is Hard

It challenges your sense of control. When your partner pursues big dreams, it often means you can't predict or control how your life will change.

It triggers insecurity. Her growth might highlight areas where you feel stagnant or inadequate.

It requires sacrifice. Supporting someone else's dreams often means adjusting your own plans, timeline, or comfort zone.

It brings uncertainty. Dreams don't come with guarantees, and uncertainty feels risky.

It might change the relationship dynamic. If she becomes more successful, confident, or fulfilled, the balance in your relationship might shift.

These fears are normal, but they don't have to dictate your response.

The Scarcity vs. Abundance Mindset

Scarcity thinking: There's only so much success, fulfillment, and opportunity to go around. If she gets more, I get less.

Abundance thinking: Success, growth, and fulfillment aren't zero-sum games. Her achievements can benefit both of us and create more opportunities for everyone.

Scarcity thinking: If she becomes more successful, she'll outgrow me.

Abundance thinking: If she becomes more successful, she'll have more to bring to our relationship, and I can learn from her example.

Scarcity thinking: Supporting her dreams might require sacrifices I'm not ready to make.

Abundance thinking: Supporting her dreams is an investment in our relationship and both of our long-term fulfillment.

What True Support Looks Like

Supporting your partner's dreams doesn't mean blindly agreeing to everything or ignoring legitimate concerns. It means approaching her ambitions with curiosity, encouragement, and collaborative problem-solving rather than fear and resistance.

True support includes:

- Getting genuinely excited about what excites her
- Asking thoughtful questions about her goals and vision
- Offering to help brainstorm solutions to obstacles
- Being willing to make reasonable sacrifices for her success
- Celebrating her achievements and milestones
- Providing emotional support during setbacks
- Adjusting your own plans when necessary to accommodate her

growth

True support doesn't mean:

- Agreeing to everything without discussion
- Ignoring how her choices affect you
- Sacrificing all your own goals for hers
- Supporting dreams that are genuinely harmful or unrealistic
- Pretending you don't have concerns or fears

Real-World Example: The Business Launch

When Carmen decided to quit her corporate job to start her own marketing consultancy, her husband Luis had serious concerns. They had a mortgage, two young children, and Carmen's corporate salary was higher than his.

Instead of immediately opposing the idea, Luis asked Carmen to help him understand her vision: "What would success look like for you? What's your timeline for replacing your corporate income? How can we manage the financial risk during the transition?"

Together, they created a plan: Carmen would build her client base while still employed, save six months of expenses as a safety net, and transition gradually rather than quitting immediately.

"Luis never made me feel like my dream was foolish or selfish," Carmen explained later. "He had legitimate concerns, but he approached them as problems we could solve together rather than reasons I shouldn't pursue what I wanted."

Two years later, Carmen's business was thriving, earning more than her corporate salary had. But more importantly, their relationship had grown stronger through the process of supporting each other through a major transition.

When Her Dreams Are Bigger Than Yours

Sometimes your partner's ambitions will dwarf your own, and that can trigger deep insecurities about your own worth and contribution to the relationship.

Remember:

- Different people have different definitions of success and fulfillment
- Supporting someone else's big dreams doesn't diminish your own value
- Relationships benefit when both people are operating at their highest potential
- You don't have to match her ambition level to be worthy of her love
- Your role as a supportive partner is valuable and important

Ask yourself:

- Am I threatened by her success, or am I inspired by it?
- Do I want to be with someone who plays small to make me feel comfortable?
- How can her achievements enhance our life together?
- What would I want her to do if our situations were reversed?

The Practical Side of Dream Support

Financial planning: If her dreams require financial investment, work together to create a realistic plan that doesn't jeopardize your security.

Timeline coordination: Help her think through realistic timelines that consider both her goals and your shared responsibilities.

Skill development: Encourage her to develop the skills she needs for success, and offer to support her learning process.

Network building: Help her connect with people who can support her goals, or attend networking events together.

Emotional support: Be her safe harbor during the inevitable setbacks and challenges that come with pursuing meaningful goals.

Practical support: Take on additional household or family responsibilities when she needs time to focus on her dreams.

When Dreams Conflict

Sometimes her dreams will directly conflict with yours, and you'll need to navigate these tensions together:

Career timing: She wants to go back to school when you were hoping to start a family.

Location: Her dream job is in a different city from where you want to live.

Risk tolerance: She wants to start a business when you prefer financial security.

Time allocation: Her goals require significant time that would reduce your time together.

Approach these conflicts with:

- Open communication about both of your needs and concerns
- Creative problem-solving to find solutions that honor both perspectives
- Willingness to compromise and make trade-offs
- Professional guidance (therapy, coaching) if you're stuck
- Acceptance that sometimes there are no perfect solutions

Real-World Example: The PhD Decision

When Patricia got accepted to a PhD program in another state, she and her partner Jordan faced a difficult decision. Jordan had a thriving career in their current city and wasn't excited about relocating.

Instead of one person sacrificing completely for the other, they got creative: Patricia would start the program, and Jordan would keep their current job while visiting regularly. After the first year, they'd reassess and decide whether Jordan would relocate permanently.

"It wasn't perfect," Jordan admitted, "but it felt fair. We were both making sacrifices, and we were both invested in making it work."

The arrangement worked for both of them. Patricia thrived in her program, and Jordan eventually found an even better career opportunity in the new city.

Supporting Dreams vs. Enabling Delusions

There's a difference between supporting legitimate dreams and enabling unrealistic fantasies:

Support dreams when:

- She has a realistic plan and timeline
- She's willing to put in the necessary work
- The dream aligns with her skills and interests
- She's prepared for the challenges and setbacks
- The pursuit doesn't harm your family's wellbeing

Be cautious about:

- Dreams with no concrete plan or realistic timeline
- Goals that require ignoring obvious obstacles or limitations

- Pursuits that would cause serious financial or emotional harm
- Dreams that seem more about escaping current problems than pursuing positive goals

You can be supportive while still asking practical questions and raising legitimate concerns.

The Long-Term Benefits

When you actively support your partner's dreams:

She feels valued and understood. Knowing that you want her to succeed makes her feel loved and appreciated for who she really is.

Your relationship grows stronger. Facing challenges together and celebrating successes together creates deeper intimacy and partnership.

You both benefit from her success. Her achievements often create opportunities and benefits for both of you.

You become more attractive. Confident, successful people are drawn to partners who support their growth rather than limit it.

You learn and grow too. Supporting someone else's dreams often inspires you to pursue your own more boldly.

Your relationship becomes more resilient. Couples who navigate major changes together develop skills that help them handle future challenges.

When You're the One with Smaller Dreams

Not everyone wants to conquer the world, and that's perfectly fine. But if your partner is highly ambitious and you're more content with stability, here's how to maintain a healthy dynamic:

Own your choices. Don't apologize for wanting a quieter life, but don't resent her for wanting more.

Find your own sources of fulfillment. You don't have to match her career ambitions, but you should have things that excite and motivate you.

Appreciate different strengths. Maybe she's the visionary and you're the steady foundation. Both roles are valuable.

Communicate your needs. Let her know what you need to feel valued and connected in the relationship.

Avoid becoming a hindrance. Even if you don't share her ambitions, don't become the person who holds her back.

Supporting Dreams That Scare You

Sometimes the dreams that most need your support are the ones that frighten you most:

Her dream of traveling the world solo might trigger fears about safety and independence.

Her goal of starting a business might challenge your need for financial security.

Her desire to go back to school might change the timeline for other life goals.

Her ambition to take on a leadership role might shift your relationship dynamic.

Remember:

- Your fears are valid, but they shouldn't dictate her choices
- Growth often requires moving through discomfort
- The alternative to supporting her dreams might be losing her entirely
- You can express your concerns while still being supportive

The Cheerleader vs. Partner Balance

Supporting her dreams doesn't mean becoming just a cheerleader who applauds from the sidelines. You're still a partner with legitimate needs and opinions.

Effective partners:

- Celebrate her successes genuinely
- Offer practical help and support
- Provide honest feedback when asked
- Share their own concerns respectfully
- Maintain their own identity and goals
- Negotiate compromises when dreams conflict

Ineffective partners:

- Only support dreams that don't threaten their comfort zone
- Use "practical concerns" to discourage her from pursuing goals
- Make her choose between her dreams and the relationship
- Become resentful when her success requires sacrifices
- Lose themselves completely in supporting her goals

Creating a Dream-Supportive Relationship

Regular check-ins: Make time to discuss each other's goals, progress, and changing priorities.

Shared vision: Work together to create a vision for your life that includes both of your dreams.

Flexible planning: Accept that supporting big dreams often requires adjusting timelines and plans.

Celebrate together: Make her successes feel like wins for both of you.

Learn together: Let her achievements inspire your own growth and goal-setting.

Key Takeaways

- Supporting your partner's dreams, even when they're bigger than yours, strengthens relationships
- Fear of change and insecurity about your own worth can make it hard to be genuinely supportive
- True support involves practical help, emotional encouragement, and collaborative problem-solving
- Different-sized dreams don't make either person less valuable in the relationship
- Sometimes supporting dreams requires sacrifices, compromises, and moving through discomfort
- The alternative to supporting her growth might be losing her entirely
- Relationships thrive when both people are operating at their highest potential

Action Steps

1. **Examine Your Fears:** Think about your partner's current goals or dreams. What fears or concerns do they trigger for you? Are these fears based on realistic concerns or insecurities?
2. **Have the Dreams Conversation:** Ask your partner about her biggest goals and aspirations. Listen without immediately jumping to practical concerns or obstacles.
3. **Identify Support Opportunities:** Think about concrete ways you could support her current goals. What practical help could you offer? What sacrifices might be required?

4. **Address Your Own Dreams:** Make sure you have goals and aspirations of your own. If you don't, start developing them.

5. **Practice Abundance Thinking:** Next time you feel threatened by her success or ambitions, consciously shift to thinking about how her achievements could benefit both of you.

6. **Plan Together:** If she has a major goal she's pursuing, work together to create a realistic plan that addresses both her dreams and your legitimate concerns.

The women in your life don't need you to have bigger dreams than they do. They need you to be genuinely excited about their dreams, to help them overcome obstacles, and to celebrate their successes as if they were your own.

That's not just supportive—it's the foundation of a partnership that grows stronger over time rather than more limiting.

When you support someone's dreams, you're not just helping them achieve their goals. You're demonstrating that you see their full potential, that you want them to become everything they're capable of becoming, and that you're excited to be part of their journey.

That kind of support doesn't just build better relationships—it builds better people.

IV

Intimacy and Connection

10

Intimacy Starts Outside the Bedroom

"He wants to be physically intimate, but he hasn't been emotionally intimate with me all week."

This frustration from Elena captures one of the most common disconnects in relationships: the assumption that physical intimacy can exist independently from emotional intimacy.

Many men compartmentalize these two types of connection, thinking they can ignore the emotional relationship for days or weeks and then expect physical intimacy to be readily available. But for most women—and increasingly for men too—physical intimacy is deeply connected to emotional intimacy, trust, and feeling genuinely connected to their partner.

If you want a satisfying physical relationship, you need to understand that it's built on a foundation of emotional connection, daily kindness, genuine interest, and consistent care.

The Intimacy Ecosystem

Think of intimacy as an ecosystem where everything is connected. Physical intimacy doesn't exist in isolation—it's supported by:

Emotional intimacy: Feeling close, understood, and emotionally safe with each other

Intellectual intimacy: Sharing thoughts, ideas, and meaningful conversations

Spiritual intimacy: Connecting on values, purpose, and deeper meaning

Recreational intimacy: Having fun together and sharing enjoyable experiences

Daily intimacy: Small moments of connection, attention, and care throughout regular life

When these other forms of intimacy are strong, physical intimacy tends to flow naturally. When they're weak or missing, physical intimacy often suffers—no matter how much you might want it or how attracted you are to each other.

Real-World Example: The Weekend Pattern

Jason couldn't understand why his girlfriend Meredith seemed less interested in physical intimacy lately. From his perspective, nothing had changed—he still found her attractive, still initiated regularly, still enjoyed their time together.

But when Meredith explained her experience, Jason realized he'd been missing crucial context:

"During the week, Jason is completely focused on work," Meredith said. "He comes home, we talk about logistics—dinner, weekend plans, who's doing what—and then he watches TV or scrolls his phone. We barely have real conversations. He doesn't ask about my day in any meaningful way, doesn't share what's going on with him, doesn't seem particularly interested in connecting with me as a person."

"Then Friday night comes, and suddenly he wants to be physically intimate. It feels like he sees me as a convenience rather than a person he's genuinely connected to."

Jason's problem wasn't that he didn't care about Meredith—he loved her deeply. His problem was that he wasn't building emotional intimacy throughout the week, then expecting physical intimacy to be available on demand.

The Daily Deposits

Think of emotional connection like a bank account. Every interaction either makes a deposit (building intimacy) or a withdrawal (creating distance). Physical intimacy requires a positive balance in the emotional intimacy account.

Daily deposits include:

- Asking genuine questions about her day and actually listening to the answers
- Sharing something real about your own experience
- Offering comfort when she's stressed or upset
- Showing interest in things that matter to her
- Being fully present during conversations instead of multitasking
- Physical affection that doesn't lead to sex (hugs, kisses, touching)
- Expressing appreciation for who she is, not just what she does
- Making eye contact and really seeing her

Daily withdrawals include:

- Being dismissive or distracted when she tries to connect

133

- Criticizing or being consistently negative
- Ignoring her emotional needs or concerns
- Only showing physical affection when you want sex
- Being on your phone during conversations
- Taking her for granted or not acknowledging her contributions
- Being consistently grumpy, stressed, or emotionally unavailable

The Foreplay That Happens All Day

Many people think foreplay is something that happens right before sex. But real foreplay—the kind that creates genuine desire and connection—happens throughout the day, week, and relationship.

Emotional foreplay includes:

- Sending a thoughtful text during the day
- Remembering something important she mentioned and asking about it
- Doing something considerate without being asked
- Having a conversation that makes her feel heard and understood
- Making her laugh or sharing a moment of genuine connection
- Showing appreciation for who she is as a person
- Being emotionally available and supportive

When you consistently make these emotional deposits, physical intimacy becomes a natural extension of your connection rather than something you have to negotiate or convince her to participate in.

The Presence Factor

One of the most important gifts you can give your partner is your genuine presence—your full attention and emotional availability.
Being present means:

- Putting away distractions when you're together
- Making eye contact during conversations
- Responding to what she's actually saying rather than thinking about your response
- Noticing her moods and energy levels
- Being emotionally available rather than shut down or distracted

Not being present includes:

- Checking your phone while she's talking
- Watching TV during dinner conversations
- Being physically there but mentally elsewhere
- Going through the motions of listening without really engaging
- Being consistently preoccupied with work, stress, or other concerns

Small Gestures, Big Impact

Intimacy is built through accumulation of small, consistent acts of care and attention:

Morning connections: How you start the day together sets a tone. A genuine "good morning," a kiss goodbye, or asking about her plans shows care.

Thoughtful texts: A message during the day that shows you're thinking of her (not just logistics or requests).

Evening reunions: When you see each other after work, do you greet each other warmly? Ask about each other's day? Or just dive into household management?

Bedtime rituals: How you end the day together matters. Do you connect before sleep, or just collapse into bed scrolling phones?

Weekend attention: Do you use downtime to connect with each other, or just pursue individual activities?

Real-World Example: The Transformation

When Marcus realized that emotional intimacy was connected to physical intimacy, he decided to experiment with increasing his daily emotional deposits.

Instead of coming home and immediately checking his phone, he started greeting his wife Chloe with genuine attention: "How was your day? You look tired—was work stressful?"

He began asking follow-up questions: "How did the presentation go?" "Is your boss still being unreasonable about that project?"

He started sharing more about his own day too, not just the facts but his feelings: "I was frustrated in that meeting today. I felt like nobody was listening to my ideas."

Within a few weeks, Chloe noticed the change: "It felt like Marcus was actually interested in my life again, not just going through the motions of being in a relationship."

The result? Their physical intimacy improved dramatically, not because Marcus was trying to get more sex, but because they were genuinely more connected as people.

The Emotional Safety Connection

Physical intimacy requires vulnerability, and vulnerability requires safety. If someone doesn't feel emotionally safe with you, they're not going to feel comfortable being physically vulnerable.

Emotional safety includes:

· Knowing you won't mock or dismiss her feelings
· Trusting that you're genuinely interested in her wellbeing
· Feeling confident that you see her as a whole person, not just a source of physical gratification
· Knowing that you care about her pleasure and comfort, not just your own
· Feeling respected and valued for who she is

Threats to emotional safety:

· Criticism or mockery during vulnerable moments
· Pressure or guilt about physical intimacy
· Only showing affection when you want something
· Being dismissive of her concerns or feelings
· Making her feel like a sexual object rather than a person

The Attention Economy

We live in an age of constant distraction, which makes genuine attention more valuable than ever. When you give someone your full attention, you're giving them something increasingly rare and precious.

Quality attention includes:

- Looking at her when she's talking
- Asking questions that show you're engaged
- Remembering details from previous conversations
- Being curious about her thoughts and experiences
- Making her feel like the most interesting person in the room

This kind of attention is intimacy-building because it communicates that she matters to you, that you find her interesting, and that you want to understand her inner world.

Beyond Physical: The Other Intimacies

Intellectual intimacy: Sharing ideas, having meaningful conversations, being curious about each other's thoughts and opinions.

Creative intimacy: Experiencing art, music, books, or creative projects together. Sharing what moves or inspires you.

Adventure intimacy: Trying new experiences together, exploring places, taking on challenges as a team.

Spiritual intimacy: Connecting on deeper questions of meaning, purpose, values, and what matters most.

Playful intimacy: Having fun together, being silly, laughing, engaging in activities that bring out your joy.

Each of these creates connection and builds the foundation for physical intimacy.

The Communication Bridge

Often, the path to better physical intimacy goes through better communication about intimacy itself:

Talk about your connection: "I feel most connected to you when..." "I love it when you..."

Share your needs: "I'd love more physical affection throughout the day, not just when we're being sexual."

Discuss timing and context: "I find it hard to feel intimate when I'm stressed about work. Can we talk about that?"

Express appreciation: "I loved how present you were during dinner tonight. It made me feel really connected to you."

Real-World Example: The Check-In Ritual

Brian and Keisha developed what they called "evening check-ins"—ten minutes each evening where they sat together without phones and asked each other: "How are you feeling right now? What do you need from me tonight?"

Sometimes the answer was "I need to vent about work." Sometimes it was "I'm exhausted and just need quiet time together." Sometimes it was "I'm feeling disconnected and would love some affection."

"It sounds simple," Keisha explained, "but it made such a difference. Instead of guessing what each other needed or getting frustrated when our needs didn't align, we just started asking."

This simple ritual improved their overall intimacy dramatically because they were consistently checking in with each other's emotional and physical needs.

The Rejection Reframe

When physical intimacy doesn't happen, many men interpret this as personal rejection. But often, it's not about you—it's about the context, timing, or emotional climate.

Instead of thinking: "She doesn't want me."

Try thinking: "What does she need right now? How can I help her feel more connected/relaxed/safe?"

This shift from taking rejection personally to being curious about her experience often leads to better outcomes for both of you.

Common Intimacy Killers

The transaction mindset: "I did dishes, so now she should want to be intimate." Intimacy isn't earned through chore completion.

The pressure approach: Making her feel guilty or pressured about frequency or timing of physical intimacy.

The neglect-then-expect pattern: Ignoring emotional connection all week, then expecting physical connection on demand.

The performance focus: Being so focused on sexual performance that you miss the emotional connection.

The routine trap: Letting physical intimacy become so routine that it loses emotional meaning.

Building Sustainable Intimacy

Consistency matters more than intensity: Daily small connections are more important than occasional grand gestures.

Quality over quantity: Better to have fewer but more meaningful intimate encounters than frequent but disconnected ones.

Emotional maintenance: Regularly tend to your emotional connection, not just when you want physical intimacy.

Communication as foreplay: Meaningful conversations are one of the most effective ways to build desire and connection.

Patience with the process: Building intimacy is ongoing work, not a problem to be solved once.

The Long-Term Benefits

When you consistently build emotional intimacy:

Physical intimacy improves naturally: When people feel connected, they naturally want more physical closeness.

Both people feel more satisfied: Intimacy based on genuine connection is more fulfilling than intimacy based on routine or obligation.

The relationship feels more alive: Regular emotional connection keeps relationships feeling fresh and engaging.

Trust deepens: Consistent emotional care builds the safety needed for vulnerability.

Conflicts decrease: People who feel consistently connected have fewer relationship conflicts.

Advanced Intimacy Skills

Reading emotional temperature: Learning to sense when your partner is open to connection vs. when they need space.

Creating rituals: Developing consistent ways to connect that work for both of you.

Balancing needs: Negotiating different intimacy needs without anyone feeling pressured or neglected.

Maintaining mystery: Staying interesting and mysterious even in long-term relationships.

Growing together: Allowing your intimate connection to evolve as you both change and grow.

Key Takeaways

- Physical intimacy is deeply connected to emotional intimacy for most people
- Daily small acts of connection and care build the foundation for physical intimacy
- Presence and genuine attention are among the most intimate gifts you can give
- Emotional safety is required for physical vulnerability
- Different types of intimacy (emotional, intellectual, spiritual) all support physical connection
- Consistent emotional deposits matter more than occasional grand gestures
- Communication about intimacy needs can dramatically improve your physical relationship

Action Steps

1. **Track Your Daily Deposits:** For one week, notice how many daily emotional deposits you make versus withdrawals. Are you building connection or creating distance?
2. **Practice Presence:** Choose one interaction per day to be completely present—no phone, no distractions, full attention on your partner.
3. **Start an Evening Check-In:** Implement a brief daily ritual where you ask each other: "How are you feeling? What do you need from me tonight?"
4. **Increase Non-Sexual Physical Affection:** Make an effort to be physically affectionate without it leading to sex. Hold hands, hug, kiss, touch her shoulder when you walk by.
5. **Have the Intimacy Conversation:** Talk with your partner about

what makes her feel most connected to you and what creates desire for physical intimacy.

6. **Expand Your Intimacy Types:** Choose one other type of intimacy (intellectual, creative, spiritual) to focus on developing with your partner.

The women in your life want to feel connected to you as a person before they feel connected to you physically. They want to know that you're interested in their minds, their feelings, their experiences—not just their bodies.

When you consistently make emotional deposits through genuine care, attention, and interest, physical intimacy becomes a natural expression of your connection rather than something you have to negotiate or convince.

That's not just better for your sex life—it's better for your entire relationship.

11

The Truth About Physical Intimacy

"I wish he understood that good sex starts with feeling like he actually wants to connect with me, not just my body."

This insight from Jasmine gets to the heart of one of the most misunderstood aspects of relationships: what actually creates satisfying physical intimacy for women.

Many men approach physical intimacy with assumptions learned from movies, porn, or locker room conversations rather than from actual communication with real partners. The result is often a disconnect between what men think women want physically and what women actually experience as satisfying, connecting, and desirable.

This chapter isn't a technical manual—it's about understanding the emotional and relational context that makes physical intimacy meaningful and satisfying for both people.

The Context Is Everything

For most women, the quality of physical intimacy is deeply influenced by the context in which it happens:

The emotional context: How connected do you feel as a couple?

Have you been emotionally intimate recently, or has it been days of just logistics and surface interaction?

The relational context: Does she feel respected, appreciated, and cared for in the relationship overall? Or does physical intimacy feel like the only time you show her focused attention?

The timing context: Is this happening when she's relaxed and receptive, or when she's stressed, tired, or preoccupied with other concerns?

The communication context: Do you talk about physical intimacy openly and comfortably, or is it something that just "happens" without discussion?

The safety context: Does she feel emotionally and physically safe with you? Can she express her needs and boundaries without fear of judgment or pressure?

When these contexts are positive, physical intimacy tends to be more satisfying for both people. When they're problematic, even technically skilled physical interaction can feel disconnected or unsatisfying.

Real-World Example: The Saturday Morning Difference

Trevor noticed that physical intimacy with his girlfriend Isabella was much better on weekend mornings than at other times, and he couldn't figure out why.

When he asked Isabella about it, her explanation was revealing: "Saturday mornings are when we're both relaxed, we've usually had coffee and talked about our week, and I'm not thinking about work or all the things I need to do. You're more present too—you're not rushing or distracted. It feels like you actually want to be with me, not just release physical tension."

This helped Trevor understand that the quality of their physical connection was directly related to their emotional connection and the absence of external stressors. The physical techniques weren't different—but the context was completely different.

Communication Is the Foundation

One of the biggest barriers to satisfying physical intimacy is the assumption that you should already know what your partner wants without having to discuss it.

This assumption leads to:

- Repeating the same approaches whether they work or not
- Missing cues about what she enjoys or doesn't enjoy
- Anxiety about performance rather than focus on connection
- Frustration when things don't go as expected
- Guessing instead of knowing what creates pleasure for her specifically

Open communication creates:

- Better understanding of each other's preferences and boundaries
- More confidence and less anxiety for both people
- Opportunities to learn and improve together
- Greater emotional intimacy through vulnerable sharing
- More satisfying experiences because you know what actually works

The Pressure Problem

Nothing kills desire faster than pressure—whether it's pressure to perform, pressure to want physical intimacy when you're not in the mood, or pressure to respond in specific ways.

Pressure shows up as:

- Making her feel guilty when she's not in the mood
- Expecting physical intimacy to follow a predictable schedule
- Taking it personally when she needs a different approach or timing
- Focusing more on your own satisfaction than on mutual enjoyment
- Being goal-oriented rather than focused on the experience itself

Reducing pressure means:

- Accepting that desire naturally fluctuates for both people
- Being interested in her experience, not just your own
- Creating space for "no" without guilt or punishment
- Focusing on connection and pleasure rather than specific outcomes
- Understanding that good physical intimacy often requires patience and presence

Real-World Example: The Frequency Frustration

When Austin and Rebecca started living together, Austin noticed that their physical intimacy became less frequent. His initial reaction was to feel rejected and to start initiating more often, which only made Rebecca feel more pressured.

The breakthrough came when Austin shifted his focus from frequency to quality: "Instead of worrying about how often we were being intimate, I started paying attention to whether Rebecca actually seemed to be enjoying our time together."

Austin realized that when he focused on creating emotional connection and reducing pressure, Rebecca was naturally more interested in physical intimacy. "When I stopped keeping score and started focusing on making sure she felt good, everything improved."

147

Understanding Desire Differences

Men and women often experience desire differently, and understanding these differences can improve physical intimacy for both people:

Spontaneous desire: Feeling aroused and wanting physical intimacy seemingly out of nowhere. This is often portrayed as the "normal" way to experience desire, but it's actually just one type.

Responsive desire: Becoming aroused and interested in physical intimacy in response to emotional connection, physical touch, or romantic context. This is equally normal and healthy.

Many women experience more responsive desire, which means they may not feel spontaneously interested in physical intimacy but can become very interested when the right emotional and physical conditions are present.

This means:

- Physical intimacy might need to start with emotional connection and non-sexual touch
- Creating the right context is often more important than perfect technique
- Patience and presence matter more than persistence
- Her seeming "less interested" might just mean she needs different conditions to access her desire

The Pleasure Focus

Many men are goal-oriented in their approach to physical intimacy, focusing on specific outcomes rather than on mutual pleasure and connection.

Goal-oriented approaches:

- Focusing primarily on achieving orgasm (yours or hers)
- Following a predictable sequence of activities
- Treating foreplay as something to get through rather than enjoy
- Measuring success by frequency or specific outcomes
- Being more concerned with performance than connection

Pleasure-focused approaches:

- Being curious about what feels good for both of you
- Taking time to explore and enjoy the entire experience
- Communicating during intimate moments about what's working
- Being present with physical sensations rather than focused on what's next
- Measuring success by how connected and satisfied you both feel

The Emotional Component

For many women, physical pleasure is closely connected to emotional connection. This doesn't mean they can't enjoy purely physical experiences, but the best physical intimacy often happens when both people feel emotionally connected.

Emotional connection during physical intimacy includes:

- Eye contact and presence rather than distraction or performance anxiety
- Verbal communication about what feels good or what you want
- Attention to her emotional state and comfort level
- Expressing affection and care, not just physical desire
- Being responsive to her cues and needs in the moment

Real-World Example: The Communication Game-Changer

When Gabriel and Sofia were having issues with physical intimacy, their therapist suggested they try spending time together naked without any expectation of sexual activity—just talking, cuddling, and being comfortable with physical closeness.

"It was awkward at first," Sofia admitted, "but it helped us get comfortable with communication and physical intimacy without the pressure of performance."

This exercise helped them start talking more openly about what they enjoyed, what they wanted to try, and what wasn't working. "Once we could talk about it openly, everything got so much better," Gabriel explained. "I finally understood what Sofia actually enjoyed instead of just guessing."

Quality Over Quantity

Many couples get caught up in frequency rather than focusing on the quality of their physical connection.

High-quality physical intimacy includes:

- Both people feeling genuinely interested and present
- Open communication about preferences and boundaries
- Attention to emotional connection as well as physical pleasure
- Time and patience rather than rushing through the experience
- Mutual satisfaction and care for each other's experience

Low-quality physical intimacy might include:

- One or both people going through the motions without genuine interest

- Lack of communication about what's working or not working
- Focus on individual satisfaction rather than mutual pleasure
- Rushing or pressure to reach specific outcomes
- Feeling disconnected even during physical closeness

The Individual Approach

What works for one woman won't necessarily work for another. Rather than assuming you know what all women want, focus on learning what your specific partner enjoys.

This means:

- Asking her directly about her preferences and boundaries
- Paying attention to her responses and reactions
- Being willing to try new approaches and adapt based on feedback
- Understanding that her preferences might change over time
- Not taking your approach from previous partners as a blueprint for current ones

Creating Safety for Communication

Many people feel shy or awkward talking about physical intimacy, even with long-term partners. Creating safety for these conversations is crucial.

Safe communication includes:

- Having these conversations outside the bedroom when you're both relaxed
- Being non-judgmental about preferences and boundaries
- Expressing curiosity rather than criticism
- Being open about your own preferences and insecurities

- Making it clear that her comfort and pleasure are priorities for you

The Timing Factor

When and how you initiate physical intimacy can significantly impact your partner's receptiveness and enjoyment.

Consider:

- Her energy level and stress state
- Whether you've had emotional connection recently
- The timing in relation to other activities and responsibilities
- Her natural rhythms and preferences for when she feels most interested
- Whether you're both present and focused or distracted by other concerns

Real-World Example: The Initiation Shift

David used to initiate physical intimacy the same way every time: late at night when they were already in bed. His wife Carmen often seemed tired or distracted, which led to frustration for both of them.

When they talked about it, Carmen explained: "By the time we're in bed, I'm exhausted from the day and thinking about everything I need to do tomorrow. I'd be much more interested if you initiated earlier in the evening when we're relaxed and connected."

David started paying attention to Carmen's energy and receptiveness rather than just following his own routine. "When I started initiating when she seemed relaxed and happy rather than when it was convenient for me, everything changed."

The Aftercare Element

What happens after physical intimacy is just as important as what happens during it.

Good aftercare includes:

- Staying emotionally connected rather than immediately moving to other activities
- Expressing affection and appreciation for the experience
- Checking in about how she's feeling
- Physical closeness and continued affection
- Making the experience feel complete rather than transactional

Common Physical Intimacy Mistakes

The routine trap: Doing the same things in the same order without variation or communication.

The pressure cooker: Making her feel guilty or pressured when she's not interested.

The performance focus: Being so concerned with technique that you miss the connection.

The assumption game: Assuming you know what she wants without asking or paying attention to her responses.

The goal obsession: Being so focused on specific outcomes that you miss the journey.

The emotional disconnect: Treating physical intimacy as separate from emotional intimacy.

Building Better Physical Connection

Start with emotional connection: Make sure you're connected as people before trying to connect physically.

Communicate openly: Talk about preferences, boundaries, and desires outside of intimate moments.

Focus on pleasure: Pay attention to what feels good for both of you rather than following a script.

Be present: Stay mentally and emotionally present during physical intimacy rather than getting distracted or anxious.

Take your time: Allow physical intimacy to develop naturally rather than rushing to specific outcomes.

Stay curious: Continue learning about your partner's preferences and how they might change over time.

When Physical Intimacy Isn't Working

Sometimes couples struggle with physical intimacy despite good intentions and emotional connection:

Possible factors:

- Medical issues that affect desire or comfort
- Past trauma that impacts physical vulnerability
- Medication effects on libido or physical response
- Stress, depression, or anxiety affecting desire
- Unresolved relationship issues creating emotional barriers

When to seek help:

- When communication alone doesn't resolve ongoing issues
- When one or both people are experiencing distress about your

physical relationship
- When medical factors might be involved
- When past trauma is affecting current intimacy

The Long-Term Perspective

Physical intimacy in long-term relationships naturally evolves and changes. What matters most is maintaining connection, communication, and mutual care rather than expecting things to stay exactly the same.

Healthy long-term physical intimacy includes:

- Adapting to life changes and stressors together
- Continuing to communicate about changing needs and preferences
- Maintaining emotional connection as the foundation
- Being patient with natural fluctuations in desire and frequency
- Growing together rather than growing apart

Key Takeaways

- Context (emotional, relational, timing) dramatically affects the quality of physical intimacy
- Communication about physical intimacy is essential and should happen outside the bedroom
- Pressure is one of the biggest killers of desire and satisfaction
- Many women experience responsive rather than spontaneous desire
- Quality matters more than frequency for long-term satisfaction
- Each person's preferences are individual and may change over time
- Physical intimacy is deeply connected to emotional intimacy and overall relationship health

Action Steps

1. **Have the Conversation:** Ask your partner about her preferences, boundaries, and what makes physical intimacy most enjoyable for her. Share your own thoughts too.
2. **Focus on Context:** Pay attention to when your partner seems most receptive and interested. What contexts create the best experiences?
3. **Practice Presence:** During your next intimate moment, focus on being completely present rather than goal-oriented or performance-focused.
4. **Reduce Pressure:** Notice if you create pressure around frequency or performance. Work on accepting "no" gracefully and focusing on quality over quantity.
5. **Expand Your Definition:** Think about physical intimacy more broadly—including non-sexual touch, cuddling, massage, and other forms of physical connection.
6. **Check In Regularly:** Make it a habit to ask how your partner is feeling about your physical relationship and whether there's anything she'd like to be different.

Physical intimacy at its best is an expression of emotional connection, trust, and mutual care. When you approach it with genuine interest in your partner's experience, good communication, and focus on connection rather than performance, it becomes a source of bonding and pleasure for both of you.

The women in your life want to feel desired as whole people, not just as physical bodies. They want physical intimacy to be an expression of your emotional connection, not separate from it.

That understanding—that physical intimacy is about connection, communication, and mutual pleasure rather than performance or routine—will transform not just your physical relationship, but your entire relationship.

12

Maintaining Mystery While Being Transparent

"I want to know everything about him, but I also want him to keep surprising me."

This seemingly contradictory desire from Olivia captures one of the most delicate balances in long-term relationships: how to be completely open and honest with your partner while still maintaining the intrigue and mystery that keeps attraction alive.

Many couples struggle with this balance. Some swing toward total transparency, sharing every thought and feeling until there's no privacy or mystery left. Others maintain so much independence and mystery that they never achieve genuine intimacy. The healthiest relationships find a way to be deeply authentic while still preserving individual identity and the capacity to surprise each other.

The Transparency-Mystery Paradox

Transparency builds trust and intimacy: When you're open about your thoughts, feelings, fears, and experiences, it creates emotional safety and deep connection. Your partner feels like they truly know you.

Mystery maintains attraction and interest: When someone remains somewhat unpredictable, continues growing and changing, and maintains their own identity, it keeps the relationship feeling fresh and dynamic.

The key is understanding that these aren't opposite forces—they're complementary aspects of a healthy relationship.

What Healthy Transparency Looks Like

Healthy transparency doesn't mean sharing every random thought or eliminating all personal boundaries. It means being genuine, honest, and emotionally available while still maintaining your individual identity.

Healthy transparency includes:

- Sharing your genuine feelings about important matters
- Being honest about your fears, hopes, and insecurities when appropriate
- Expressing your needs and boundaries clearly
- Admitting when you're wrong or when you've made mistakes
- Being authentic about your values and what matters to you
- Sharing your inner world without overwhelming your partner

Unhealthy transparency includes:

- Sharing every fleeting thought or emotion without filter
- Using honesty as an excuse to be hurtful or inconsiderate
- Overwhelming your partner with constant emotional processing
- Sharing intimate details about your relationship with others
- Being so open that you lose all personal boundaries
- Making your partner responsible for managing all your emotions

What Healthy Mystery Looks Like

Healthy mystery isn't about being secretive or manipulative. It's about maintaining your individual identity, continuing to grow and evolve, and preserving some aspects of yourself that unfold over time.
Healthy mystery includes:

- Having your own interests and hobbies that don't involve your partner
- Continuing to learn and grow as an individual
- Maintaining friendships and relationships outside your partnership
- Having thoughts and experiences that you don't immediately share
- Surprising your partner with new sides of yourself
- Preserving some independence and individual identity

Unhealthy mystery includes:

- Being secretive about important matters
- Hiding things that directly affect your partner
- Creating artificial distance or unavailability
- Refusing to be vulnerable or emotionally open
- Maintaining mystery through deception or withholding
- Using mystery to manipulate or control your partner

Real-World Example: The Photography Surprise

When Nathan started taking photography classes, he didn't immediately tell his girlfriend Zoe about it. Not because he was hiding it, but because he wanted to see if he was actually good at it before making a big deal about it.

Three months later, when Nathan had developed real skill and passion for photography, he surprised Zoe by showing her his portfolio and suggesting they take a photography trip together.

"I was so impressed," Zoe said later. "Not just by his photos, but by the fact that he'd been quietly developing this whole new side of himself. It made me realize there were still things about Nathan I didn't know, which was exciting."

This is healthy mystery: Nathan wasn't hiding his photography to be secretive, but he was allowing a new aspect of himself to develop privately before sharing it. The surprise enhanced their relationship rather than threatening it.

The Evolution Factor

One of the best ways to maintain mystery while being transparent is to continue evolving as a person. When you're actively growing, learning, and changing, you'll naturally have new things to share and new aspects of yourself to reveal.

Personal evolution includes:

- Learning new skills or exploring new interests
- Reading books that change your perspective
- Having experiences that challenge your assumptions
- Developing new aspects of your personality
- Setting and pursuing personal goals
- Reflecting on your values and priorities

When you're actively evolving, transparency doesn't eliminate mystery because there's always something new emerging.

The Individual Identity Balance

Many couples make the mistake of merging their identities completely, which eliminates mystery but also eliminates the individual growth that keeps relationships interesting.

Healthy couples:

- Maintain their own friendships and interests
- Have some separate experiences and activities
- Continue growing as individuals while also growing as a couple
- Support each other's individual development
- Celebrate each other's unique qualities and perspectives

Unhealthy couples:

- Do everything together and have no separate experiences
- Lose their individual identities in the relationship
- Stop growing as individuals once they're coupled
- Feel threatened by their partner's independent interests
- Expect their partner to meet all their social and emotional needs

Real-World Example: The Book Club Decision

When Victoria wanted to join a book club, her husband Peter's first reaction was to suggest they find one they could join together. But Victoria gently explained that she wanted something that was just hers.

"I love sharing things with Peter," Victoria said, "but I also wanted to have my own intellectual space where I could explore ideas and make friends independently."

Peter initially felt a little left out, but he came to appreciate having a partner who was intellectually stimulated and growing. "Victoria comes home from book club excited about new ideas, and she's more interesting to talk to because she's engaging with people and concepts outside our relationship."

This is the balance: Victoria was completely transparent about wanting individual space and growth, but she used that space to become more interesting and engaged as a partner.

The Timing of Transparency

Not everything needs to be shared immediately. Sometimes the most transparent thing you can do is take time to process your thoughts and feelings before sharing them.

Immediate sharing works well for:

- Feelings that directly affect your partner
- Important decisions that impact both of you
- Concerns about the relationship
- Daily experiences and updates
- Appreciation and positive feelings

Processing before sharing works well for:

- Complex emotions you don't fully understand yet
- Work stress or external problems you're still working through
- Ideas or plans that are still forming
- Feelings that might be temporary or situational
- Personal growth insights that need time to develop

Predictability vs. Reliability

There's an important difference between being predictable and being reliable:

Reliability is attractive: Your partner can count on you to follow through on commitments, be supportive during difficulties, and maintain consistent care and respect.

Predictability can be boring: If your partner always knows exactly what you're going to say, do, or think, the relationship can start feeling stagnant.

The goal is to be reliably supportive but unpredictably interesting.

Real-World Example: The Surprise Date Tradition

Marcus and Ava developed a tradition where once a month, one of them would plan a surprise date for the other. The catch was that it had to be something they'd never done together before.

"We were completely transparent about the fact that we were planning surprise dates," Ava explained, "but the content of the dates remained mysterious until they happened."

This created a structure for planned surprises that maintained mystery while being completely honest about the intention to surprise each other.

The Growth Mindset in Relationships

When both people in a relationship are committed to personal growth, it naturally creates ongoing mystery because you're both continuously becoming new versions of yourselves.

Growth-minded couples:

- Encourage each other's personal development
- Share what they're learning about themselves
- Celebrate each other's achievements and changes
- Adapt to each other's evolving needs and interests
- See change as opportunity rather than threat

This approach means that even after years together, you're still discovering new things about your partner because they're still discovering new things about themselves.

The Privacy Boundaries

Even in the most transparent relationships, everyone needs some degree of privacy. The key is being clear about what kind of privacy is healthy versus what might be secretive or harmful.

Healthy privacy might include:

- Time alone to think and process
- Some friendships that don't involve your partner
- Personal journaling or reflection time
- Individual interests and hobbies
- Private conversations with family members about non-relationship matters

Unhealthy secrecy might include:

- Hiding financial decisions or problems
- Concealing communications with ex-partners
- Being secretive about whereabouts or activities
- Lying about or omitting important information
- Hiding behaviors that would concern your partner

The difference is usually whether the privacy serves individual growth and health versus avoiding accountability or deceiving your partner.

Maintaining Intrigue in Daily Life

Long-term relationships can fall into routines that eliminate mystery and surprise. Here are ways to maintain intrigue while being completely honest:

Vary your routines: Don't do everything the same way every time.

Continue learning: Take classes, read books, explore new ideas that you can share.

Plan surprises: Small, thoughtful surprises show that you're thinking about your partner in new ways.

Ask new questions: Even after years together, there are always new things to learn about someone.

Share your inner world gradually: You don't have to reveal everything about yourself immediately; let some things unfold over time.

The Emotional Availability Balance

Being emotionally available doesn't mean being emotionally available 24/7. Sometimes the most caring thing you can do is take time to process your emotions privately so you can share them more thoughtfully.

Healthy emotional availability:

- Being present when your partner needs support
- Sharing your emotional world when it affects the relationship
- Processing your own emotions so you can be supportive to others
- Being vulnerable when it builds intimacy
- Taking care of your emotional health so you can be a good partner

Real-World Example: The Career Change Contemplation

When Jordan started feeling dissatisfied with his career, he didn't immediately share every doubt and worry with his wife Hannah. Instead, he took some time to really think through what he was feeling and what he might want to do about it.

After a few weeks of reflection, Jordan sat down with Hannah and said, "I've been doing some thinking about my career, and I'd love to talk through some ideas with you."

"I appreciated that Jordan took time to process before involving me in his emotional journey," Hannah explained. "He was completely honest about what he was going through, but he'd done enough thinking that our conversation could be productive rather than just him dumping anxiety on me."

This is the balance: being transparent about important matters while also being thoughtful about timing and presentation.

The Long-Term Relationship Challenge

The longer you're with someone, the more challenging it becomes to maintain mystery while being transparent. But this challenge is also an opportunity:

Years 1-2: Everything is mysterious because you're still learning about each other.

Years 3-7: The challenge is maintaining mystery as you become very familiar with each other.

Years 8+: The opportunity is becoming mysterious to each other in new ways as you both continue to grow and evolve.

The couples who thrive long-term are those who see familiarity as a foundation for deeper exploration rather than an end to discovery.

Creating Space for Surprise

Give each other permission to change: Don't lock your partner into being exactly who they were when you met them.

Ask new questions: "What's something you've been thinking about lately that you haven't shared?"

Encourage individual growth: Support your partner's interests and development even when they don't directly benefit you.

Plan surprises: Create opportunities to surprise each other within the context of your honest, transparent relationship.

Share your evolution: Be open about how you're growing and changing as a person.

The Communication Balance

Daily sharing: Share the basic facts and feelings about your day-to-day life.

Weekly deeper sharing: Have more substantial conversations about what's going on in your inner world.

Monthly reflection: Take time to reflect on how you're both growing and what you're discovering about yourselves and each other.

Seasonal planning: Look ahead at goals, dreams, and changes you might want to make.

Common Mistakes

The over-sharer: Sharing every thought and feeling without filter, overwhelming your partner with information.

The mystery manipulator: Creating artificial mystery through withholding, secretiveness, or game-playing.

The merger: Completely losing individual identity in the relationship.

The compartmentalizer: Keeping so much private that your partner never feels like they really know you.

The static partner: Stopping all personal growth once you're in a relationship.

Advanced Skills

Reading the room: Knowing when your partner is open to deeper sharing versus when they need lighter interaction.

Gradual revelation: Sharing deeper aspects of yourself over time rather than all at once.

Supporting mystery: Encouraging your partner's individual growth and interests even when they don't directly involve you.

Dynamic transparency: Adapting how much you share based on your partner's capacity and the relationship's needs.

Key Takeaways

- Transparency and mystery aren't opposites—they're complementary aspects of healthy relationships
- Healthy transparency means being genuine and honest, not sharing every random thought
- Healthy mystery comes from continued growth and individual identity, not secretiveness
- The key is being reliably supportive but unpredictably interesting
- Both people need some degree of privacy and individual space to maintain their identity
- Long-term relationships require ongoing effort to maintain intrigue and discovery
- Personal growth naturally creates ongoing mystery as you continue

to evolve

Action Steps

1. **Assess Your Current Balance:** Are you sharing too much, too little, or in a healthy balance? Are you maintaining individual interests and growth?
2. **Develop Individual Interests:** Choose one new hobby, skill, or area of learning that's just for you. Explore it independently before sharing it with your partner.
3. **Plan a Surprise:** Create one small surprise for your partner this week. It doesn't have to be big—just something thoughtful and unexpected.
4. **Ask New Questions:** This week, ask your partner questions you've never asked before. What are they curious about? What would they like to try?
5. **Practice Thoughtful Sharing:** Next time you have something complex to share, take time to process it first so you can share it thoughtfully rather than just dumping raw emotion.
6. **Encourage Their Mystery:** Support your partner in developing an interest or pursuing a goal that doesn't directly involve you.

The goal isn't to become a mysterious, unknowable person. The goal is to be genuinely transparent about who you are while continuing to grow and evolve as an individual within your partnership.

The women in your life want to know the real you—your thoughts, feelings, fears, and dreams. But they also want to continue discovering new aspects of who you are as you grow and change over time.

That's not contradiction—that's the foundation of relationships that stay alive, interesting, and connected for the long term.

V

The Long Game

13

Love Languages Are Just the Beginning

"I kept giving him what I thought he wanted, and he kept giving me what he thought I wanted, but we were both missing the mark."

This realization from Stephanie captures why so many well-intentioned couples struggle despite genuinely caring for each other. They're trying to show love and care, but they're not speaking each other's emotional language.

Most people have heard of love languages—the idea that people prefer to receive love through words of affirmation, acts of service, receiving gifts, quality time, or physical touch. This framework has helped millions of couples better understand each other's needs. But it's just the beginning of understanding how to create deep, lasting connection.

Real relationship mastery involves understanding not just how your partner prefers to receive love, but how they process emotions, handle stress, make decisions, and navigate the world. It's about becoming fluent in the language of your specific partner, not just love languages in general.

Beyond the Basic Five

The original love languages framework gives you five broad categories, but real people are much more nuanced than that. Your partner might prefer:

Words of affirmation, but specifically:

- Appreciation for things she does rather than just general compliments
- Recognition of her intelligence and capabilities rather than just her appearance
- Private affirmation rather than public praise
- Written notes she can keep rather than spoken words

Quality time, but specifically:

- Uninterrupted conversation rather than just being in the same room
- Shared activities rather than passive time together
- Regular one-on-one time rather than group activities
- Adventure and new experiences rather than routine time together

Physical touch, but specifically:

- Casual affection throughout the day rather than just intimate moments
- Massage and soothing touch when she's stressed
- Hand-holding and arm-linking in public
- Playful touch rather than always romantic touch

The framework gives you a starting point, but your job is to learn the specific ways your partner experiences and interprets care.

Real-World Example: The Acts of Service Miscommunication

When Ryan learned that his girlfriend Melanie's love language was acts of service, he started doing more household tasks—washing dishes, taking out trash, organizing her closet. But Melanie didn't seem to feel more loved.

The problem wasn't that acts of service wasn't her love language—it was that Ryan was focusing on the wrong kinds of service. Through conversation, Ryan learned that Melanie felt most cared for when he:

- Remembered things that were important to her and followed up on them
- Anticipated her needs when she was stressed or overwhelmed
- Took care of tasks that required planning and mental energy, not just physical work
- Did things that made her life easier rather than just keeping the house clean

"I realized that 'acts of service' for Melanie wasn't about housework— it was about thoughtfulness and reducing her mental load," Ryan explained later. "Once I understood that, I could actually help her feel loved."

Understanding Attachment Styles

Beyond love languages, understanding attachment styles can dramatically improve your relationship skills. Attachment styles describe how people learned to connect with others in early relationships, and they significantly affect adult romantic relationships.

Secure attachment (about 50% of people):

- Comfortable with intimacy and independence
- Good at communicating needs directly
- Able to offer and receive support effectively
- Generally trusting and emotionally stable in relationships

Anxious attachment (about 20% of people):

- Craves closeness but worries about being abandoned
- May become clingy or demanding when feeling insecure
- Often needs frequent reassurance about the relationship
- Can be very giving but may expect constant reciprocation

Avoidant attachment (about 25% of people):

- Values independence and can be uncomfortable with too much closeness
- May withdraw when partner seeks more intimacy
- Often has difficulty expressing emotions or needs
- Generally self-reliant but may struggle with vulnerability

Disorganized attachment (about 5% of people):

- Inconsistent patterns of seeking and avoiding closeness
- May have experienced trauma or inconsistent caregiving
- Can be unpredictable in their relationship needs
- Often benefits from professional support

Understanding these patterns helps you recognize that your partner's relationship behaviors aren't just personal preferences—they're often rooted in deep psychological patterns developed early in life.

Real-World Example: The Reassurance Discovery

When Chloe started dating Trevor, she noticed he needed frequent reassurance about their relationship. At first, she found it flattering, but eventually it became exhausting.

"Trevor would ask me multiple times a day if I still loved him, if I was happy, if I was thinking about breaking up," Chloe explained. "I started to feel like nothing I said was ever enough."

When they learned about attachment styles, everything made more sense. Trevor had anxious attachment, which meant he genuinely needed more reassurance than Chloe (who had secure attachment) naturally wanted to give.

Instead of getting frustrated, Chloe learned to give Trevor reassurance proactively: "I started telling him I loved him before he asked, and sending him texts during the day that let him know I was thinking about him. When I gave him reassurance before his anxiety kicked in, he actually needed less of it overall."

This wasn't about accommodating unhealthy neediness—it was about understanding Trevor's attachment style and finding ways to help him feel secure so he could show up as his best self in the relationship.

Stress Styles and Response Patterns

People handle stress very differently, and understanding your partner's stress patterns is crucial for supporting them effectively.

Some people handle stress by:

- Talking through their problems and emotions
- Seeking physical comfort and reassurance
- Wanting practical help solving problems
- Needing space and time to process alone
- Engaging in physical activity or movement
- Seeking distraction through entertainment or social activity

Your partner's stress response might be:

- Becoming more talkative and emotional
- Becoming quiet and withdrawn
- Getting more organized and controlling
- Becoming scattered and unfocused
- Seeking more physical affection
- Avoiding physical touch when overwhelmed

Learning how your partner specifically handles stress allows you to offer support in ways that actually help rather than accidentally making things worse.

Decision-Making Styles

Understanding how your partner makes decisions can prevent count-less conflicts and misunderstandings:
Some people make decisions by:

- Gathering lots of information and analyzing options carefully
- Going with their gut feelings and intuition
- Consulting with friends and family for input
- Making quick decisions and adjusting as needed
- Avoiding decisions until they absolutely have to be made

- Making decisions collaboratively with their partner

When decision-making styles clash:

- Quick deciders can feel frustrated by slow, analytical partners
- Intuitive deciders might feel overwhelmed by partners who need lots of data
- Collaborative deciders might feel excluded by partners who decide independently
- Avoiders might feel pressured by partners who want immediate decisions

Real-World Example: The Vacation Planning Revelation

When planning their first big vacation together, Marcus and Lauren discovered they had completely different decision-making styles.

Marcus liked to research thoroughly—reading reviews, comparing prices, and making detailed itineraries. Lauren preferred to pick a destination and figure things out when they got there.

Initially, they both felt frustrated. Marcus thought Lauren was being irresponsible; Lauren thought Marcus was being controlling.

The breakthrough came when they recognized these were just different approaches, not right and wrong ways to plan. They developed a system: Marcus would do the initial research and present Lauren with three good options. Lauren would pick the one that felt most exciting to her, and Marcus would handle the logistics while leaving room for spontaneous activities.

"Once we understood how each other's minds worked, we could collaborate instead of fighting," Lauren explained.

Communication Styles Under Pressure

People's communication styles often change dramatically when they're stressed, upset, or feeling pressured. Understanding these patterns can help you navigate difficult conversations more effectively.

Under stress, some people:

- Become more direct and blunt
- Become more emotional and expressive
- Shut down and stop talking
- Become more aggressive or defensive
- Seek more reassurance and validation
- Need more time to process before responding

Recognizing these patterns helps you:

- Adjust your approach when your partner is stressed
- Avoid taking stress-responses personally
- Know when to push for resolution versus when to give space
- Offer the right kind of support during difficult times

Energy Management Styles

Understanding how your partner manages their energy can improve your daily interactions and prevent misunderstandings:

Introverts typically:

- Recharge through alone time or quiet activities
- Prefer deeper conversations with fewer people
- May need transition time when coming home from work
- Can feel drained by too much social stimulation

- Often think before speaking

Extroverts typically:

- Recharge through social interaction and activity
- Enjoy meeting new people and trying new experiences
- May want to talk through their day immediately when they come home
- Can feel energized by social stimulation
- Often think out loud while speaking

Ambiverts (most people) have characteristics of both and may:

- Need social time and alone time in different proportions
- Have energy patterns that vary based on circumstances
- Adapt their social needs based on stress levels and life situations

Real-World Example: The After-Work Adjustment

Jake (an extrovert) and Priya (an introvert) struggled with their after-work routine. Jake wanted to talk about his day immediately when he got home, while Priya needed 30 minutes to decompress before engaging in conversation.

Initially, Jake felt rejected when Priya didn't want to talk, and Priya felt overwhelmed by Jake's immediate need for interaction.

Once they understood their different energy patterns, they created a routine that worked for both: When they got home, Priya would have 30 minutes of quiet time while Jake would call a friend or family member. Then they'd come together for dinner and conversation when Priya was ready to engage.

"It wasn't that we didn't want to connect," Priya explained. "We just needed to connect in a way that worked for both of our energy styles."

Conflict Resolution Styles

People have very different approaches to handling disagreements and conflicts:

Some people prefer to:

- Address conflicts immediately when they arise
- Take time to cool down before discussing issues
- Talk through problems extensively until they're resolved
- Solve practical problems and let emotional issues fade
- Bring in outside perspectives to help resolve conflicts
- Avoid conflict altogether and hope issues resolve themselves

Understanding your partner's conflict style helps you navigate disagreements more effectively and avoid the common trap of assuming your approach is the "right" one.

Learning Your Partner's Language

Observe patterns: Pay attention to when your partner seems happiest, most stressed, most connected, and most distant. What patterns do you notice?

Ask direct questions: "What makes you feel most loved?" "How do you prefer to handle stress?" "What kind of support do you find most helpful?"

Experiment and adjust: Try different approaches and pay attention to your partner's responses. What seems to work best?

Have ongoing conversations: People's needs and preferences can change over time, especially during different life stages or stress levels.

Don't assume your way is universal: Just because something works for you doesn't mean it works for your partner.

Beyond Love Languages: The Complete Picture

Appreciation language: How does your partner prefer to be appreciated and recognized?

Comfort language: How does your partner want to be comforted when they're upset or stressed?

Motivation language: What motivates your partner to pursue goals or make changes?

Processing language: How does your partner prefer to work through problems or decisions?

Connection language: What makes your partner feel most connected to you day-to-day?

The Cultural and Family Context

Your partner's emotional language is also influenced by:

Family patterns: How did her family express love, handle conflict, and communicate?

Cultural background: What cultural values and communication styles influence her expectations?

Past relationships: What has she learned about relationships from previous experiences?

Life experiences: How have major life events shaped her emotional needs and responses?

Understanding this context helps you appreciate why certain things are particularly important to your partner and why some approaches might trigger unexpected reactions.

Adapting Your Natural Style

Learning to speak your partner's emotional language often means adapting your natural communication style:

If you're naturally direct and she's more sensitive to tone: Practice softer approaches without losing your authenticity.

If you're naturally reserved and she needs more emotional expression: Work on being more openly affectionate and appreciative.

If you're naturally solution-focused and she needs emotional support first: Practice listening and validating before jumping to problem-solving.

If you're naturally spontaneous and she needs more planning: Build in more structure while still leaving room for spontaneity.

When Languages Don't Match

Sometimes you and your partner will have very different emotional needs and communication styles. This doesn't mean you're incompatible—it means you need to become bilingual.

Successful couples learn to:

- Appreciate different approaches rather than judging them
- Compromise by meeting each other's needs part of the time
- Communicate about their different styles openly
- Find creative solutions that work for both people
- Accept that perfect matching isn't necessary for great relationships

The Long-Term Evolution

Your partner's emotional language may evolve over time due to:

Life stage changes: New parents have different needs than empty nesters

Stress level changes: High-stress periods may change what kinds of support are most helpful

Personal growth: As people develop and mature, their emotional needs may shift

Relationship security: As trust builds, people may become comfortable with different kinds of connection

Successful long-term relationships require ongoing attention to how your partner's needs and communication styles may be changing.

Advanced Emotional Intelligence

Reading microexpressions: Learning to notice subtle changes in facial expression and body language.

Understanding emotional sequences: Recognizing the patterns of how your partner's emotions typically unfold.

Timing awareness: Knowing when your partner is most receptive to different kinds of communication.

Context sensitivity: Understanding how environment and circumstances affect your partner's emotional state.

Repair skills: Knowing how to reconnect when you've misread signals or approached something incorrectly.

Key Takeaways

- Love languages are a useful starting point, but each person's emotional needs are much more nuanced
- Attachment styles significantly influence how people experience and express love in relationships
- Understanding stress responses, decision-making styles, and energy patterns improves daily interactions
- Your partner's emotional language is influenced by family, culture, and life experiences
- Successful relationships require learning to "speak" your partner's specific emotional language
- Emotional languages can evolve over time and need ongoing attention
- Being bilingual in relationships means adapting your style while staying authentic

Action Steps

1. **Identify Attachment Styles:** Learn about attachment styles and try to identify both your own and your partner's. How do these patterns show up in your relationship?
2. **Study Stress Patterns:** Observe how your partner handles stress and what kind of support they find most helpful. Ask them directly about their preferences.
3. **Map Decision-Making Styles:** Notice how you and your partner make decisions differently. Where do your styles complement each other, and where do they create friction?
4. **Understand Energy Patterns:** Pay attention to your partner's energy rhythms. When are they most social vs. when do they need alone time?

5. **Have the Language Conversation:** Ask your partner: "What makes you feel most loved and appreciated? What kind of support do you find most helpful when you're stressed?"
6. **Practice Adaptation:** Choose one area where you can better adapt to your partner's communication style while staying authentic to yourself.

The goal isn't to become a completely different person or to accommodate every preference your partner has. The goal is to become fluent enough in your partner's emotional language that you can connect with them effectively and support them in ways that actually feel supportive.

The women in your life want to be understood not just as women, but as the specific, unique individuals they are. Learning their particular emotional language—how they process stress, express love, handle conflict, and navigate the world—is one of the most valuable relationship skills you can develop.

That understanding transforms you from someone who's trying generic relationship advice to someone who knows exactly how to connect with the person you love.

14

When Life Gets Real

"Anyone can be a good partner when things are going well. What matters is how you show up when everything falls apart."

This wisdom from relationship therapist Dr. Sue Johnson captures a fundamental truth: the real test of a relationship isn't how you handle the good times—it's how you navigate the inevitable storms that life throws at every couple.

Job losses, health crises, family emergencies, financial stress, mental health struggles, the death of loved ones, infertility, career setbacks, and countless other challenges will test your relationship. The couples who thrive long-term aren't the ones who avoid difficulties—they're the ones who learn to face challenges as a team.

The Reality of Adult Life

Early in relationships, most challenges are relationship-focused: learning to communicate, navigating differences, building trust and intimacy. But as relationships mature, external pressures become major factors:

Career pressures: Job stress, unemployment, career transitions, work-life balance struggles

Health issues: Chronic illness, mental health challenges, injuries, aging parents

Financial stress: Debt, unexpected expenses, economic downturns, differing money values

Family drama: Difficult relatives, caregiving responsibilities, grief and loss

Life transitions: Moving, having children, empty nest syndrome, retirement

External crises: Natural disasters, economic crashes, global pandemics, community trauma

These challenges can either strengthen relationships by bringing couples closer together, or destroy them by creating overwhelming stress and conflict.

The Partnership vs. Individual Stress Response

When facing major life challenges, people often revert to individual coping strategies rather than partnership approaches. This is natural but can be relationship-damaging.

Individual stress responses:

- Withdrawing emotionally to protect yourself
- Focusing solely on your own needs and survival
- Making decisions unilaterally without consulting your partner
- Blaming your partner for additional stress or inadequate support
- Shutting down communication to avoid more conflict or pressure

Partnership stress responses:

- Communicating openly about fears, needs, and concerns

- Making decisions together even when it's more difficult
- Supporting each other's different ways of coping with stress
- Sharing practical and emotional labor during difficult times
- Protecting the relationship even while managing external pressures

The couples who navigate challenges successfully learn to choose partnership responses even when individual responses feel easier or more natural.

Real-World Example: The Job Loss Crisis

When Derek lost his job unexpectedly, his first instinct was to withdraw from his wife Aria and handle the crisis alone. He spent days applying for jobs without telling her about rejections, canceled social plans without explanation, and became increasingly irritable and distant.

Aria felt shut out and confused. "Derek was clearly struggling, but every time I tried to support him, he pushed me away. I started to feel like I was the enemy instead of his partner."

The turning point came when Derek's best friend pointed out what was happening: "You're treating Aria like she's another problem to manage instead of a resource for getting through this."

Derek realized he needed to shift from individual crisis mode to partnership mode. He sat down with Aria and explained what he was going through: his fears about money, his anxiety about career prospects, and his shame about being unemployed.

"Once Derek let me in on what he was experiencing, I could actually support him," Aria said. "We made a plan together, divided up job search tasks, and figured out how to manage our finances during the transition. Instead of Derek handling unemployment alone while I worried from the sidelines, we handled it as a team."

Derek found a new job six weeks later, but more importantly, they both learned how to face major challenges together.

The Stress Amplification Factor

Major life stress doesn't just add pressure to relationships—it amplifies existing weaknesses and reveals underlying problems that might otherwise remain manageable.
Stress amplifies:

- Communication problems that are minor during good times
- Different values and priorities that don't usually cause conflict
- Individual coping mechanisms that might clash under pressure
- Financial disagreements that are dormant when money isn't tight
- Different needs for support, space, or connection during difficult times

This is why couples who seem perfectly compatible during easy times sometimes struggle or break up when facing major challenges. The stress reveals incompatibilities or weak spots that were always there but hadn't been tested.

Building Stress Resilience Together

Create a support plan before you need it: Discuss how you want to handle major challenges before they arise. What kind of support does each person need? How will you make decisions during crises?

Establish communication protocols: Agree on how you'll keep each other informed during stressful times, even when you're both overwhelmed.

Build financial resilience: Having emergency savings and clear financial plans reduces stress and provides more options during difficult times.

Develop individual coping skills: Each person should have healthy ways to manage stress that don't depend entirely on their partner.

Strengthen your support network: Maintain friendships and family relationships that can provide additional support during tough times.

Practice stress management together: Develop shared strategies for managing stress—exercise, meditation, hobbies, or other activities that help you both stay grounded.

Real-World Example: The Health Crisis Partnership

When Samantha was diagnosed with breast cancer at age 35, she and her husband Connor faced the biggest challenge of their five-year marriage. The diagnosis brought immediate stress: medical decisions, treatment logistics, financial concerns, and emotional upheaval.

Instead of trying to handle everything themselves, Samantha and Connor immediately activated their support network. Connor's parents helped with household management, Samantha's sister researched treatment options, and their friends organized meal deliveries.

But more importantly, they developed a system for handling the ongoing stress together:

Daily check-ins: Each morning, they spent ten minutes discussing the day's medical appointments, emotional needs, and practical tasks.

Shared decision-making: All treatment decisions were made together after gathering information and discussing options.

Individual support: Connor joined a support group for partners of cancer patients, and Samantha worked with a therapist specializing in medical trauma.

Maintaining connection: They protected time for non-cancer conversations and activities, ensuring their relationship didn't become entirely focused on illness.

"Cancer was horrible," Samantha reflected two years later, "but it also showed us how well we could work together under pressure. We came out of it closer than we'd ever been."

Supporting Without Fixing

One of the biggest challenges when your partner is facing difficulties is the urge to fix everything rather than simply being supportive.

The fixing approach:

- Immediately jumping into solution mode
- Taking over tasks or decisions to reduce your partner's burden
- Getting frustrated when your solutions aren't welcomed
- Feeling responsible for your partner's emotional state
- Pushing for quick resolution rather than accepting the process

The supporting approach:

- Asking what kind of support would be most helpful
- Offering practical help without taking over completely
- Providing emotional support even when you can't solve the problem
- Accepting that some difficulties require time to resolve
- Maintaining your own emotional stability while supporting your partner

The goal is to be a supportive partner, not a rescuer or problem-solver-in-chief.

Different Coping Styles

People handle major stress in very different ways, and these differences can create additional relationship stress if not understood and respected:

Some people cope by:

- Talking through their feelings and concerns extensively
- Seeking distraction through work, hobbies, or entertainment
- Wanting extra physical comfort and reassurance
- Needing more alone time to process and recharge
- Becoming more organized and controlling to manage anxiety
- Seeking support from friends, family, or professionals

Understanding your partner's coping style helps you:

- Offer the right kind of support rather than the kind you would want
- Avoid taking their coping mechanisms personally
- Support their healthy coping strategies even if they're different from yours
- Recognize when professional help might be beneficial

Real-World Example: The Parent Care Dilemma

When Isabella's father was diagnosed with dementia, she wanted to talk through every decision and emotion with her partner Miguel. Miguel's instinct was to research practical solutions and handle logistics efficiently.

Initially, this created friction. Isabella felt like Miguel wasn't emotionally available, while Miguel felt overwhelmed by Isabella's need to process everything verbally.

The solution came when they recognized their different coping styles and found ways to honor both:

- Miguel handled research and logistics, giving Isabella detailed updates without requiring her to manage these tasks herself
- Isabella processed emotions with a therapist and close friends, reducing the pressure on Miguel to be her primary emotional support
- They scheduled weekly check-ins to make decisions together and ensure they were both informed and involved

"We learned that we could support each other better by accepting our different strengths rather than expecting each other to cope the same way," Miguel explained.

Maintaining Connection During Crisis

When facing major challenges, couples often focus so much on managing the crisis that they neglect their relationship. But maintaining connection during difficult times is crucial for long-term relationship health.

Ways to maintain connection:

- Protect some time for non-crisis conversations and activities
- Continue showing affection and appreciation for each other
- Acknowledge the stress you're both under and how well you're handling it
- Maintain physical intimacy at whatever level feels appropriate
- Remember to laugh together when possible
- Express gratitude for your partner's support and efforts

The Growth Opportunity

While no one wants to face major life challenges, these experiences can strengthen relationships in powerful ways:
Shared adversity can create:

- Deeper trust and intimacy from supporting each other through difficulty
- Better communication skills developed under pressure
- Greater appreciation for your partner and your relationship
- Increased confidence in your ability to handle future challenges together
- Stronger bond from having survived and overcome difficulties as a team

But only if you handle the challenges in partnership rather than as competing individuals.

When Professional Help Is Needed

Some life challenges are too big to handle without professional support:
Consider professional help when:

- The stress is affecting your mental or physical health significantly
- You're having trouble communicating or making decisions together
- One or both of you are struggling with depression, anxiety, or other mental health issues
- The challenge involves complex issues like addiction, trauma, or serious illness
- You're repeatedly having the same conflicts without resolution

- The stress is threatening your relationship stability

Seeking help isn't a sign of weakness—it's a sign of wisdom and commitment to your relationship.

Financial Stress Specifically

Money problems are one of the most common sources of relationship stress, and they require particular care:
During financial difficulties:

- Be completely transparent about the financial situation
- Make spending and saving decisions together
- Focus on creative solutions rather than blame
- Distinguish between temporary lifestyle adjustments and permanent changes
- Maintain some small pleasures within your budget constraints
- Remember that your worth as people isn't determined by your financial situation

Health Challenges

When one or both partners face health issues, the relationship dynamic inevitably changes:
The healthy partner may need to:

- Take on additional practical responsibilities
- Provide emotional support while managing their own fears
- Maintain their own health and well-being to be able to help
- Accept changes in the relationship dynamic without resentment

The partner with health issues may need to:

- Communicate their needs clearly rather than expecting their partner to guess
- Accept help gracefully without feeling guilty about being a "burden"
- Maintain as much independence as possible within their limitations
- Express appreciation for their partner's increased efforts

Career and Life Transitions

Major life transitions—job changes, moves, having children, retirement—require renegotiation of roles and expectations:
During transitions:

- Communicate openly about fears and excitement regarding the changes
- Renegotiate household and financial responsibilities as needed
- Support each other's adjustment to new circumstances
- Be patient with the process of adapting to change
- Maintain flexibility as you figure out new routines and dynamics

Building Anti-Fragile Relationships

Some relationships are fragile—they break under stress. Some are resilient—they can withstand stress and return to their original state. The strongest relationships are anti-fragile—they actually get stronger when faced with challenges.
Anti-fragile relationships:

- Use challenges as opportunities to deepen trust and intimacy
- Learn from difficulties and become better partners as a result
- Develop systems and skills that help them handle future challenges more effectively
- View obstacles as things they face together rather than threats to their relationship

Long-Term Perspective

Remember that most major life challenges are temporary, even when they don't feel that way in the moment:

- Job loss is usually followed by finding new employment
- Health crises often have periods of recovery and stability
- Financial difficulties can be resolved with time and effort
- Family emergencies eventually stabilize
- Even major losses can be integrated into a meaningful life over time

Maintaining perspective helps you make decisions that protect your long-term relationship rather than just managing immediate crisis.

Key Takeaways

- Major life challenges test relationships more than daily conflicts or compatibility issues
- The key is responding to stress as a partnership rather than reverting to individual survival mode
- Different people have different healthy coping mechanisms that should be respected
- Maintaining relationship connection during crisis requires inten-

tional effort
- Many challenges can strengthen relationships if handled well
- Professional help is often beneficial during major life stresses
- Building resilience before crisis hits makes couples better equipped to handle difficulties

Action Steps

1. **Discuss Your Crisis Plan:** Talk with your partner about how you want to handle major challenges before you face them. What kind of support does each person need? How will you make decisions during stressful times?

2. **Build Your Support Network:** Cultivate relationships with friends, family, and professionals who could provide support during difficult times.

3. **Develop Individual Coping Skills:** Each person should have healthy stress management strategies that don't rely entirely on their partner.

4. **Practice Partnership During Small Stresses:** Use minor challenges as opportunities to practice supporting each other and making decisions together.

5. **Create Financial Resilience:** Build emergency savings and discuss how you would handle financial difficulties together.

6. **Identify Professional Resources:** Know what professional support is available in your community for various types of crises.

Life will test your relationship with job loss, health scares, family crises, financial stress, and countless other challenges. The couples who thrive aren't the ones who avoid difficulties—they're the ones who face them together.

The women in your life don't need you to prevent all problems or fix everything that goes wrong. They need you to be a reliable partner who faces challenges alongside them, communicates openly during difficult times, and remains committed to the relationship even when everything else feels uncertain.

That's not just being a good partner during crisis—that's building the kind of relationship that becomes stronger rather than weaker when tested by real life.

15

Growing Old Together (And Still Liking Each Other)

"We're not the same people who fell in love fifteen years ago, and that's the best thing that could have happened to us."

This reflection from Patricia, married for three decades, captures something many couples struggle to understand: successful long-term relationships aren't about finding the perfect person and staying exactly the same together. They're about growing and changing in ways that keep you interesting to each other and aligned in your values and life direction.

The couples who thrive over decades understand that people evolve, priorities shift, bodies age, and circumstances change. Instead of fighting these natural processes or mourning the loss of who they used to be, they learn to grow intentionally together while still maintaining their individual identities.

The Evolution Reality

People change significantly over the course of long relationships. The person you're with at 25 will be different at 35, 45, 55, and beyond. Their interests may shift, their career ambitions might evolve, their relationship needs could change, and their perspective on life will likely mature and deepen.

Common changes over time:

- Career priorities and ambitions
- Physical health and energy levels
- Social needs and friendship patterns
- Family responsibilities and roles
- Financial values and security concerns
- Recreational interests and hobbies
- Spiritual beliefs and life philosophy
- Communication styles and emotional needs

The question isn't whether these changes will happen—it's whether you'll grow together or grow apart.

Growing Together vs. Growing Apart

Growing together means:

- Staying curious about the person your partner is becoming
- Supporting each other's individual development
- Adapting to changes rather than resisting them
- Finding new ways to connect as you both evolve
- Sharing your own growth and changes openly
- Creating new traditions and experiences together

- Maintaining flexibility in your relationship roles and expectations

Growing apart means:

- Assuming your partner will never change or expecting them to stay exactly the same
- Resisting or resenting their evolution
- Stopping communication about your own growth and changes
- Clinging to old patterns that no longer work
- Living parallel lives without ongoing connection
- Taking each other for granted or losing curiosity about each other

Real-World Example: The Career Change Partnership

When Brandon decided to leave his corporate law job to become a high school teacher at age 42, his wife Nicole initially panicked. They'd built their lifestyle around his lawyer salary, and she was worried about finances, social status, and whether this was a midlife crisis.

But instead of fighting the change or trying to talk Brandon out of it, Nicole chose to understand what was driving his desire for change. Through many conversations, she learned that Brandon felt unfulfilled by corporate work and had always been passionate about education and working with young people.

"I realized that the man I married was someone who cared deeply about making a difference in the world," Nicole explained. "Corporate law had been paying well, but it wasn't feeding his soul. The career change was actually him becoming more himself, not less."

They adjusted their lifestyle, Nicole took on some freelance work to help with finances during the transition, and Brandon made the career change. Five years later, both agreed it was one of the best decisions they'd made.

"Brandon is so much happier and more energetic now," Nicole said. "And I discovered that I'm attracted to passionate, purpose-driven Brandon even more than I was attracted to successful-but-unhappy Brandon."

The Decades Framework

Different decades of life typically bring different challenges and opportunities for growth:

20s-30s: Foundation Building

- Establishing careers and financial stability
- Learning relationship skills and communication
- Possibly starting families
- Building friend networks and social connections
- Developing individual identities within the partnership

30s-40s: Achievement and Expansion

- Career advancement and professional development
- Parenting responsibilities and family focus
- Home ownership and community involvement
- Balancing individual goals with family needs
- Managing increased responsibilities and time pressures

40s-50s: Reevaluation and Renewal

- Midlife reflection on priorities and purpose
- Possible career changes or new directions
- Aging parents and caregiving responsibilities
- Children becoming more independent

- Renewed focus on the partnership as kids need less attention

50s-60s: Transition and Wisdom

- Empty nest adjustments
- Retirement planning and lifestyle changes
- Grandparenthood possibilities
- Health awareness and lifestyle modifications
- Deepening of spiritual or philosophical perspectives

60s+: Legacy and Fulfillment

- Retirement and new rhythms of life
- Health challenges and caregiving
- Grandparent and elder roles
- Reflection on life's meaning and accomplishments
- Facing mortality and making peace with life choices

Understanding these general patterns helps couples prepare for and navigate predictable life transitions together.

Maintaining Attraction Over Time

Physical attraction naturally changes over decades, but emotional and intellectual attraction can actually deepen:
Physical changes are inevitable:

- Bodies age, energy levels shift, health issues may arise
- Sexual needs and capabilities may evolve
- Appearance changes in ways that can't be prevented

But other forms of attraction can increase:

- Admiration for how your partner handles life challenges
- Appreciation for their wisdom and life experience
- Attraction to their competence and capabilities
- Deep emotional connection built over shared experiences
- Intellectual stimulation from their continued growth and learning

Couples who maintain attraction over time:

- Focus on what they admire about their partner's character and capabilities
- Continue to take care of themselves physically within reasonable limits
- Stay interested in each other's thoughts, dreams, and experiences
- Create new shared experiences and memories together
- Express appreciation regularly for who their partner has become

Real-World Example: The Empty Nest Renewal

After their youngest child left for college, Robert and Diane realized they'd spent twenty years being great co-parents but had somewhat lost touch with each other as romantic partners.

"We were efficient roommates who loved our kids," Diane explained. "But we realized we didn't know who each other had become during all those years of focusing on family."

Instead of accepting this as the natural progression of marriage, they decided to intentionally reconnect. They started taking weekend trips together, began asking each other deeper questions about their current thoughts and dreams, and made an effort to plan activities they both enjoyed.

"It was like dating again, but with someone I'd known for decades," Robert said. "I discovered that Diane had become even more interesting during the parenting years, not less. I just hadn't been paying attention."

Their relationship entered what they called "the second chapter"—different from their early romance, but in many ways deeper and more satisfying.

Adapting Roles and Expectations

Long-term relationships require ongoing negotiation of roles and expectations as circumstances change:

Early relationship roles might include:

- Who handles which household tasks
- How finances are managed
- Career prioritization decisions
- Social and family responsibilities

These roles may need to evolve when:

- Career situations change
- Children are born or leave home
- Health issues arise
- Aging parents need care
- Financial circumstances shift
- Personal interests and priorities change

Successful couples:

- Regularly discuss whether current arrangements are still working

- Adjust roles based on changing circumstances and capabilities
- Support each other's changing needs and priorities
- Avoid assuming that early relationship patterns must be permanent

The Friendship Foundation

Couples who thrive long-term often emphasize that they genuinely like each other as people, not just love each other romantically:
Strong friendship in marriage includes:

- Enjoying each other's company and conversation
- Respecting each other's opinions and perspectives
- Having fun together and sharing humor
- Supporting each other's individual interests and growth
- Choosing to spend time together because you enjoy it, not just because you live together

This friendship foundation helps relationships survive:

- Periods when romantic feelings are lower
- Life stresses that challenge the partnership
- Natural changes in physical attraction
- Different life stages that require adaptation

Maintaining Individual Identity

One of the biggest threats to long-term relationships is losing yourself in the partnership:
Healthy individual identity includes:

- Personal interests and hobbies
- Individual friendships and social connections
- Professional or creative pursuits that are yours alone
- Personal goals and aspirations
- Private time for reflection and renewal

This individual identity enhances rather than threatens the relationship by:

- Ensuring you have interesting things to share with your partner
- Preventing codependency and excessive neediness
- Maintaining your attractiveness as an individual person
- Providing personal fulfillment that doesn't depend entirely on the relationship

Real-World Example: The Retirement Adjustment

When George retired from his engineering career, he initially expected to spend all his time with his wife Margaret, who had been working part-time and managing most household responsibilities.

Margaret felt overwhelmed by George's sudden constant presence and his expectation that she would entertain him and provide all his social interaction.

"I loved George, but I wasn't prepared to become his full-time social director," Margaret explained. "We needed to figure out how to enjoy retirement together without losing our individual identities."

George joined a hiking group, started volunteering at a literacy center, and began pursuing photography—interests that were his own. Margaret continued her book club and volunteer work, started taking art classes, and maintained her own rhythm.

"Once we both had our own things going on, we enjoyed our together time much more," George said. "We had interesting things to share with each other, and neither of us felt like we'd lost ourselves in retirement."

Communication Evolution

The way couples communicate often needs to evolve over the decades:
Early relationship communication focuses on:

- Learning about each other's backgrounds and preferences
- Negotiating basic relationship agreements
- Managing day-to-day logistics and decisions

Long-term relationship communication includes:

- Ongoing sharing about personal growth and changing perspectives
- Regular relationship maintenance and check-ins
- Deeper conversations about life meaning and purpose
- Collaborative planning for future goals and challenges

Advanced communication skills for long-term relationships:

- Discussing difficult topics without damaging the relationship
- Supporting each other through major life transitions
- Maintaining emotional intimacy despite daily routines and familiarity
- Addressing relationship issues before they become serious problems

The Intimacy Evolution

Physical and emotional intimacy naturally changes over decades, but it doesn't have to diminish:

Physical intimacy changes may include:

- Different energy levels and timing preferences
- Health considerations that require adaptation
- Changes in desire patterns and frequency
- Need for different types of physical connection

Emotional intimacy can deepen through:

- Shared experiences of parenting, career challenges, and life transitions
- Supporting each other through difficulties and celebrating successes together
- Ongoing vulnerability and sharing about fears, dreams, and changes
- Building trust through years of reliability and mutual support

Couples who maintain strong intimacy over time:

- Adapt to physical changes without losing connection
- Continue to prioritize emotional and physical closeness
- Communicate openly about changing needs and preferences
- Create new ways to be intimate that work for their current life stage

Creating New Traditions

Long-term relationships benefit from regularly creating new traditions and experiences:

New traditions might include:

- Annual trips or adventures to places you've never been
- Regular date nights that focus on new experiences rather than routine
- Seasonal or holiday traditions that reflect your current values and interests
- Learning new skills or hobbies together
- Creating rituals that mark life transitions and anniversaries

These new experiences help prevent the relationship from becoming stagnant and give you fresh memories to build on.

Handling Major Transitions Together

Long-term relationships face predictable major transitions that require intentional navigation:

Career changes and retirement
Children leaving home
Aging parents and caregiving responsibilities
Health challenges and physical changes
Moving or lifestyle changes
Financial shifts and planning for aging

Successful transition strategies:

- Anticipating and discussing upcoming changes before they happen

- Supporting each other's adjustment to new circumstances
- Being patient with the process of adapting to change
- Seeking professional guidance when transitions are particularly challenging
- Viewing transitions as opportunities for growth rather than just obstacles

The Legacy Perspective

Couples who've been together for decades often develop a shared sense of legacy—what they've built together and what they want to leave behind:

This might include:

- Children and grandchildren they've raised
- Professional or creative achievements they've supported in each other
- Community contributions they've made together
- Home and family traditions they've created
- Lessons and wisdom they can share with younger people

This legacy perspective can provide meaning and purpose that strengthens the relationship even during difficult periods.

Avoiding the Relationship Plateau

Many long-term couples fall into comfortable but stagnant patterns:

Signs of relationship plateau:

- Conversations limited to logistics and routine matters
- Loss of curiosity about your partner's inner world

- Parallel lives with minimal genuine connection
- Assumption that you know everything about each other
- Taking the relationship for granted

Preventing plateau requires:

- Ongoing curiosity about your partner's evolving thoughts and feelings
- Regular relationship check-ins and intentional conversations
- Continuing to create new shared experiences
- Expressing appreciation and not taking each other for granted
- Treating your partner as someone who's still growing and changing

The Realistic Romance

Romance in long-term relationships looks different from new relationship romance, but it can be just as meaningful:

New relationship romance: Passion, novelty, excitement, uncertainty

Long-term relationship romance: Deep appreciation, chosen commitment, intimate knowledge, reliable love

Both are valuable, and long-term couples can maintain elements of both by:

- Continuing to choose each other daily, not just staying together out of habit
- Creating surprises and new experiences within the context of deep familiarity
- Expressing appreciation for both who your partner was and who they're becoming
- Maintaining physical affection and romantic gestures adapted to

your current life stage

Key Takeaways

- People change significantly over decades, and successful couples grow together rather than apart
- Different life stages bring predictable challenges and opportunities for growth
- Maintaining individual identity enhances rather than threatens long-term relationships
- Physical attraction changes, but emotional and intellectual attraction can deepen over time
- Communication, intimacy, and roles must evolve to match changing life circumstances
- Creating new traditions and experiences prevents relationship stagnation
- The strongest long-term relationships combine deep familiarity with ongoing curiosity and growth

Action Steps

1. **Assess Your Growth Patterns:** Discuss with your partner how you've both changed over the years. Are you growing together or starting to grow apart?
2. **Plan for Upcoming Transitions:** Look ahead at likely life changes in the next 5-10 years. How can you prepare for and navigate these together?
3. **Reconnect as Individuals:** Make sure you both maintain individual interests, friendships, and goals that keep you interesting to each other.
4. **Create New Traditions:** Plan a new experience or tradition that

reflects who you are now rather than just repeating what you've always done.

5. **Have Deeper Conversations:** Ask your partner about their current dreams, fears, and thoughts about the future. What are they thinking about that you might not know?

6. **Express Current Appreciation:** Tell your partner what you admire about who they've become, not just who they were when you first met.

The goal of a long-term relationship isn't to find the perfect person and freeze them in time. It's to find someone you can grow with, someone who makes you want to keep becoming a better version of yourself, and someone whose evolution you can support and admire.

The women in your life don't want to be taken for granted or treated like they stopped growing and changing years ago. They want partners who remain curious about who they're becoming, who support their evolution, and who continue to choose them not just out of habit but out of genuine appreciation for who they are today.

That's not just staying together—that's growing old together while still genuinely liking the people you've become.

VI

Part Six

16

The Daily Practice of Love

"Love isn't just a feeling—it's a series of actions you take every day."

This insight from relationship researcher Dr. John Gottman captures something most people don't understand about long-term relationships: love isn't just something you feel, it's something you do. And the couples who stay deeply connected over years and decades are the ones who turn love into a daily practice.

The grand gestures get the attention—proposals, anniversary trips, expensive gifts, dramatic declarations. But relationships are actually built and maintained through thousands of small, daily actions that either strengthen your bond or gradually weaken it.

This chapter is about creating sustainable daily practices that keep your relationship strong, connected, and growing, even during the routine phases of life when you're busy with work, family, and all the other demands of adult life.

The Compound Interest of Daily Actions

Small daily actions in relationships work like compound interest in finance—they seem insignificant individually, but their cumulative effect over time is transformative.

Daily withdrawal behaviors:

- Checking your phone while your partner is talking
- Coming home stressed and immediately complaining about your day
- Forgetting to acknowledge your partner's efforts or contributions
- Being consistently late or unreliable about small commitments
- Taking your partner for granted and not expressing appreciation

Daily deposit behaviors:

- Making genuine eye contact when your partner speaks
- Asking about your partner's day and really listening to the answer
- Expressing gratitude for specific things your partner does
- Following through reliably on small promises and commitments
- Offering physical affection without expecting anything in return

Over weeks and months, these small actions create either a pattern of connection or a pattern of distance.

Morning Rituals for Connection

How you start each day together sets a tone that influences your entire relationship:

Disconnected morning patterns:

- Rushing through morning routines without acknowledging each other
- Checking phones immediately upon waking
- Focusing only on logistics and schedules
- Leaving for work without meaningful goodbye contact

Connected morning patterns:

- A few minutes of genuine conversation before getting up
- Physical affection—hugging, kissing, or cuddling
- Expressing something you appreciate about your partner
- Asking about their day ahead and offering support for challenges they're facing
- A meaningful goodbye that includes eye contact and physical touch

Real-World Example: The Five-Minute Morning Revolution

When Tyler and Jasmine realized they'd been living like polite room-mates for months, they decided to implement what they called "five-minute mornings."

Before getting out of bed each day, they committed to spending five minutes connecting: sharing something they were looking forward to, expressing appreciation for each other, or just cuddling and talking about their dreams from the night before.

"It sounds so simple," Jasmine explained, "but those five minutes completely changed our relationship. Instead of starting each day focused on our individual to-do lists, we started each day focused on each other."

Tyler agreed: "It made me realize how much I'd been taking Jasmine for granted. When you start the day by intentionally connecting, you carry that feeling with you."

The Art of the Daily Check-In

Regular emotional check-ins prevent small issues from becoming big problems and help you stay connected to each other's inner worlds:
Surface-level check-ins:

- "How was your day?" (asked while distracted)
- "Fine" (response while looking at phone)
- Moving immediately to logistics or plans

Meaningful check-ins:

- "What was the best part of your day?"
- "What was challenging about today?"
- "How are you feeling about everything?"
- "What do you need from me tonight?"
- "Is there anything I can help you with?"

The key is asking questions that invite real sharing and being genuinely interested in the answers.

Evening Connection Practices

How you end each day together is just as important as how you start it:
Disconnected evening patterns:

- Collapsing in front of screens without interacting
- Focusing immediately on household tasks and logistics
- Bringing work stress home and dumping it on your partner
- Going to bed at different times without meaningful connection

Connected evening patterns:

- A transition ritual when you first see each other (hug, kiss, brief conversation)
- Device-free time for genuine conversation
- Sharing highlights and challenges from the day
- Physical affection that's not goal-oriented
- Expressing appreciation for something specific your partner did

Real-World Example: The Reunion Ritual

After Luis and Carmen noticed they'd been bringing work stress home and immediately dumping it on each other, they created what they called a "reunion ritual."

When either of them arrived home, they committed to 30 seconds of genuine connection—a real hug, eye contact, and "I'm glad you're home"—before launching into the day's problems or logistics.

"It seems like such a small thing," Luis said, "but it made a huge difference. Instead of seeing Carmen as someone to vent to about my bad day, I started seeing her as the person I was happy to come home to."

After the reunion ritual, they'd give each other 10 minutes to decompress individually before coming together to share about their days.

Weekly Relationship Maintenance

Just as you maintain your car, house, and health with regular attention, relationships need consistent maintenance:

Weekly practices might include:

- A regular date night or special time together

- A relationship check-in conversation about how things are going
- Planning something fun or meaningful for the upcoming week
- Expressing appreciation for your partner's efforts during the week
- Discussing any concerns or adjustments needed in your routines

The key is consistency: It's better to have a brief weekly check-in every week than an elaborate monthly conversation that often gets skipped.

The Appreciation Practice

One of the most powerful daily practices is actively noticing and expressing appreciation for your partner:

Instead of taking good things for granted, notice:

- Efforts your partner makes, even small ones
- Qualities you admire about your partner's character
- Things your partner does that make your life easier or better
- Ways your partner shows love or care that you might usually overlook

Express appreciation specifically:

- "I really appreciated how patient you were with the customer service rep today"
- "I love how you always remember to ask about my presentation"
- "Thank you for making coffee this morning—it was a perfect way to start the day"
- "I admire how you handled that difficult conversation with your sister"

Real-World Example: The Gratitude Experiment

When Ashley and Marcus felt like they'd been focusing too much on what bothered them about each other, they tried an experiment: for one month, they each committed to expressing one specific appreciation to their partner every day.

"At first it felt forced," Ashley admitted. "But after a few days, I started actually looking for things to appreciate instead of things to criticize."

Marcus noticed the same shift: "When I was actively looking for things Ashley did well, I started seeing so many positive things I'd been overlooking."

A month later, both reported feeling more connected and positive about their relationship. They'd retrained their brains to notice the good rather than focusing primarily on problems.

Physical Affection as Daily Practice

Non-sexual physical touch throughout the day maintains connection and intimacy:

Simple daily touches:

- Hand-holding while talking or walking
- Brief back or shoulder rubs during stressful moments
- Hugs that last longer than three seconds
- Kisses that aren't just quick pecks
- Sitting close together when watching TV or relaxing
- Brief touches while passing each other in the house

Physical affection works because:

- It releases bonding hormones like oxytocin
- It communicates care and attention without words
- It maintains physical intimacy even during busy periods
- It helps partners feel connected throughout the day

The Power of Small Surprises

Regular small surprises keep relationships feeling fresh and show that you're thinking about your partner when you're apart:

Small surprises might include:

- Bringing home your partner's favorite coffee or treat
- Leaving a loving note where they'll find it
- Sending a thoughtful text during the day
- Doing a household task they usually handle
- Planning a small activity you know they'd enjoy
- Remembering and following up on something important to them

The key is consistency rather than expense—small, regular surprises are more relationship-building than occasional grand gestures.

Creating Sacred Time

In our busy, distracted world, creating time that's protected just for your relationship connection is essential:

Sacred time characteristics:

- No phones, TV, or other distractions
- Focus entirely on each other
- Regular and protected—not just when you happen to have free time

- Used for genuine connection rather than logistics or problem-solving

Sacred time might be:

- 15 minutes of conversation before bed each night
- Saturday morning coffee together
- A weekly walk without phones
- Monthly "state of the union" relationship conversations

The Conflict Resolution Habit

Small daily practices can prevent most conflicts from escalating:
Daily conflict prevention:

- Addressing small irritations before they build up
- Expressing needs clearly rather than hoping your partner will guess
- Apologizing quickly when you make mistakes
- Giving your partner the benefit of the doubt about their intentions
- Choosing your battles and letting small things go

When conflicts do arise:

- Address them when you're both calm and have time to talk
- Focus on the specific issue rather than bringing up past grievances
- Listen to understand rather than to win
- Work toward solutions together rather than proving who's right

Seasonal Relationship Rhythms

Just as nature has seasons, relationships benefit from different rhythms throughout the year:

Spring/Summer energy: More social activities, adventures, new experiences

Fall/Winter energy: More cozy time together, deeper conversations, reflection

Create seasonal traditions:

- Summer adventures or travel
- Fall planning and goal-setting conversations
- Winter comfort rituals and cozy time
- Spring renewal activities and fresh starts

This prevents your relationship from falling into year-round sameness and gives you natural opportunities for different types of connection.

Real-World Example: The Sunday Planning Ritual

When Kevin and Sofia realized they'd been living reactively—just responding to whatever came up each day—they instituted "Sunday Planning."

Every Sunday morning over coffee, they'd spend 30 minutes looking at the upcoming week together:

- What does each person have going on?
- Where are the potential stress points?
- What do we want to prioritize for our relationship this week?
- How can we support each other through the challenging parts?
- What's one thing we want to do together this week?

"It seems so simple," Sofia explained, "but it made us feel like a team working together rather than two individuals just trying to coordinate schedules."

The Long-Term Perspective

Daily practices work because they:

Build positive momentum: Good days create good weeks, which create good months and years.

Prevent relationship drift: Regular attention prevents couples from slowly growing apart without noticing.

Create security: Consistent loving actions build trust and emotional safety.

Maintain attraction: Partners who feel appreciated and connected stay attracted to each other longer.

Build resilience: Relationships with strong daily foundations can better weather major challenges.

Common Daily Practice Mistakes

The perfection trap: Expecting to do everything perfectly every day rather than aiming for consistency over time.

The grand gesture substitution: Thinking occasional big romantic acts can replace daily attention and care.

The scorekeeper mentality: Keeping track of who does more rather than both people focusing on their own contributions.

The routine rut: Doing the same practices until they become meaningless rather than staying present and intentional.

The busy excuse: Assuming that busy periods exempt you from relationship maintenance.

Building Your Personal Daily Practice

Start small: Choose one or two practices you can realistically maintain rather than trying to overhaul everything at once.

Be consistent: Daily practices only work if you do them regularly, not just when you feel like it.

Stay flexible: Adapt your practices to different life circumstances while maintaining the underlying intention.

Make it personal: Choose practices that feel authentic to your relationship rather than copying what works for others.

Evaluate regularly: Notice what's working and what isn't, and adjust accordingly.

Advanced Daily Practices

Emotional attunement: Learning to sense your partner's emotional state and respond appropriately without being asked.

Anticipatory care: Noticing and addressing your partner's needs before they have to ask for help.

Growth support: Daily actions that support your partner's individual goals and development.

Relationship visioning: Regular conversations about your shared future and dreams.

Conflict prevention: Daily habits that address small issues before they become big problems.

The Ripple Effect

When you consistently practice love daily:

Your partner feels more valued and appreciated
You become more aware of positive aspects of your relationship

Both people are more motivated to contribute to the relationship
Small problems get addressed before becoming big ones
Your relationship becomes a source of energy rather than stress
You create a positive cycle that strengthens over time

Key Takeaways

- Love is both a feeling and a practice—successful relationships require both
- Small daily actions compound over time to create strong or weak relationship foundations
- Morning and evening rituals create positive momentum for your entire day and relationship
- Regular appreciation and physical affection maintain connection during busy periods
- Sacred time protected from distractions is essential for ongoing intimacy
- Consistency matters more than perfection in daily relationship practices
- Daily practices prevent problems and build resilience for handling major challenges

Action Steps

1. **Design Your Morning Connection:** Create a simple morning ritual that helps you start each day connected to your partner rather than just focused on individual tasks.
2. **Implement Daily Appreciation:** For the next week, express one specific appreciation to your partner every day. Notice how this affects your focus and feelings.
3. **Create Sacred Time:** Establish one period of regular, protected

time each week that's just for connecting with each other without distractions.

4. **Practice Daily Check-Ins:** Instead of surface-level "how was your day" conversations, ask more meaningful questions that invite real sharing.

5. **Add Physical Affection:** Increase non-sexual physical touch throughout the day—hand-holding, longer hugs, brief touches while passing each other.

6. **Plan Small Surprises:** Once a week, do something small and thoughtful that shows you're thinking about your partner when you're apart.

The women in your life don't need you to be romantic every day or to make grand gestures constantly. They need you to show up consistently with attention, appreciation, and care. They need to feel valued not just on special occasions, but in the ordinary moments that make up most of life.

That's not just maintaining a relationship—that's actively loving someone through your daily choices and actions. And that's what creates relationships that don't just survive, but actually get better over time.

17

Red Flags and Green Flags

"I ignored so many warning signs because I was in love with who I thought he could become instead of seeing who he actually was."

This painful realization from Katherine reflects one of the most common relationship mistakes: focusing so much on potential that you miss clear indicators of incompatibility or unhealthy behavior patterns.

Learning to recognize red flags (warning signs of problematic behavior) and green flags (indicators of healthy relationship potential) is crucial for making good relationship decisions. But it's not just about early dating—these patterns continue throughout relationships and can help you assess whether you're in a healthy dynamic or one that needs serious attention or even ending.

Understanding Red Flags vs. Deal Breakers

Red flags are warning signs that indicate potential problems. They don't automatically mean you should end a relationship, but they do mean you should pay close attention and proceed with caution.

Deal breakers are fundamental incompatibilities or behaviors that make a healthy relationship impossible. These should result in ending the relationship, regardless of other positive qualities.

The key is knowing the difference and being honest about which category certain behaviors fall into.

Early Dating Red Flags

Communication Red Flags:

- Consistently takes hours or days to respond to messages without explanation
- Gets angry when you don't respond immediately
- Refuses to have phone or video conversations, only texts
- Gives vague answers about their life, work, or past
- Makes you feel like you're bothering them when you try to communicate
- Love-bombs you with excessive attention and declarations of love very early

Boundary Red Flags:

- Pushes for physical intimacy faster than you're comfortable with
- Shows up uninvited or insists on seeing you when you've said you're busy
- Reads your texts or wants access to your social media accounts
- Gets upset when you spend time with friends or family
- Makes decisions that affect you without consulting you
- Doesn't accept "no" for an answer, even about small things

Emotional Red Flags:

- Has extreme mood swings or emotional reactions to minor situa-

tions
- Blames all their relationship problems on ex-partners
- Speaks disrespectfully about women in general or specific women in their life
- Shows little empathy for others' feelings or situations
- Needs constant reassurance or gets jealous without reason
- Makes you feel like you're walking on eggshells around them

Real-World Example: The Charming Controller

When Maya started dating Jonathan, she was impressed by how attentive he was. He texted her constantly, wanted to see her every night, and showered her with compliments and gifts.

At first, Maya felt special and desired. But gradually, she noticed concerning patterns:

- Jonathan got upset when she made plans with friends
- He would show up at her workplace "as a surprise" when she was busy
- He constantly asked where she was and who she was with
- He made negative comments about her friends and family
- He pushed for her to move in with him after only two months

"I mistook his possessiveness for passion," Maya explained later. "I thought his jealousy meant he loved me intensely. I didn't recognize that he was trying to control and isolate me."

When Maya tried to address these concerns, Jonathan's responses were more red flags:

- He turned her concerns back on her: "You're being paranoid"
- He made promises to change but nothing actually changed

- He accused her of not caring about the relationship when she asked for space
- He alternated between love-bombing and emotional withdrawal

Maya eventually ended the relationship when she realized Jonathan's behavior was becoming more controlling, not less.

Relationship Stage Red Flags

Early Relationship (Months 1-6):

- Inconsistent behavior or seems to be performing a character
- Avoids introducing you to friends or family
- Has dramatically different values on important issues
- Shows disrespect toward service workers, waitstaff, or others
- Financial irresponsibility or secrecy about money
- Substance abuse problems or concerning drinking patterns

Established Relationship (6 months+):

- Refuses to discuss the future or make commitments
- Doesn't support your goals and dreams
- Consistently makes you feel criticized or not good enough
- Has anger management issues or explosive temper
- Lies about important matters or has patterns of dishonesty
- Shows no interest in resolving conflicts or improving the relationship

Long-term/Serious Relationship:

- Refuses to seek help for obvious mental health or addiction issues

- Financial abuse or controlling behavior around money
- Emotional, verbal, or physical abuse of any kind
- Infidelity or inappropriate relationships with others
- Fundamentally different life goals that can't be compromised on
- Complete unwillingness to work on relationship problems

Green Flags: Signs of Healthy Relationship Potential

Communication Green Flags:

- Responds to messages within a reasonable timeframe
- Can have difficult conversations without becoming defensive or aggressive
- Listens actively when you speak and remembers what you've told them
- Expresses their needs clearly rather than expecting you to guess
- Apologizes sincerely when they make mistakes
- Asks questions about your life because they're genuinely interested

Character Green Flags:

- Treats service workers, family members, and strangers with respect
- Takes responsibility for their actions and doesn't blame others for their problems
- Has healthy friendships and maintains good relationships with family (when appropriate)
- Shows empathy for others and cares about people beyond themselves
- Has goals and ambitions and works toward them consistently
- Handles stress and frustration in healthy, mature ways

Relationship Green Flags:

- Shows genuine interest in your thoughts, feelings, and experiences
- Supports your individual goals and friendships
- Introduces you to their friends and family when appropriate
- Shows affection and appreciation consistently, not just when they want something
- Works to resolve conflicts constructively rather than avoiding them or escalating them
- Demonstrates trustworthiness through consistent, reliable behavior

Real-World Example: The Gradual Green Light

When Rachel started dating Carlos, she was cautious because her previous relationship had involved several red flags she'd ignored. With Carlos, she paid attention to small indicators of his character:

Early green flags Rachel noticed:

- Carlos was consistently on time and followed through on plans
- He was polite to restaurant servers and helped elderly people with heavy bags
- He asked thoughtful questions about her work and remembered details from previous conversations
- When they had their first disagreement, he listened to her perspective and worked toward a solution
- He spoke respectfully about his ex-girlfriend and took responsibility for his part in their breakup

As the relationship developed, more green flags emerged:

- Carlos encouraged Rachel's friendship with her college roommates
- He supported her decision to go back to school for her master's degree
- When Rachel's father was hospitalized, Carlos offered practical help and emotional support
- He was financially responsible and transparent about his money situation
- He introduced Rachel to his family and friends enthusiastically

"With Carlos, I didn't have to wonder where I stood or worry about his intentions," Rachel said. "His actions consistently matched his words, and I felt like he genuinely cared about my wellbeing, not just what I could do for him."

The Potential Trap

Many people stay in relationships with obvious red flags because they focus on potential rather than reality:

Common potential-focused thinking:

- "He'll change once he realizes how much I love him"
- "She's just going through a difficult time—this isn't who she really is"
- "If I'm patient and supportive enough, they'll become the person I know they can be"
- "Everyone has flaws—I need to accept them as they are"
- "The good times are so good that they make up for the bad times"

Reality-focused thinking:

- "This is who this person is right now, based on their consistent

behavior"
- "I can only make decisions based on their current actions, not their potential"
- "People can change, but only if they want to change and are actively working on it"
- "Accepting someone as they are means accepting their flaws AND their problematic behaviors"
- "Healthy relationships shouldn't have dramatic highs and lows"

Financial Red Flags

Money-related red flags often indicate deeper character issues:

Financial Red Flags:

- Hides debts, spending, or financial problems from you
- Expects you to pay for everything without contributing
- Has no savings or retirement planning despite adequate income
- Makes major financial decisions that affect both of you without consultation
- Borrows money from friends and family regularly
- Has a pattern of not paying bills on time or defaulting on obligations
- Uses money to control or manipulate you

Financial Green Flags:

- Is transparent about their financial situation when appropriate
- Shares expenses fairly based on income and circumstances
- Has realistic financial goals and works toward them
- Can discuss money matters maturely without defensiveness
- Pays their bills on time and manages debt responsibly

· Respects your financial autonomy and decision-making

Social and Family Red Flags

How someone treats the important people in their life reveals character:

Social Red Flags:

· Speaks badly about all their friends or claims to have no close friends
· Is disrespectful to your friends and family
· Isolates you from your social support network
· Has burned bridges with everyone from their past
· Shows different personalities around different people in concerning ways
· Uses information about your relationships against you during arguments

Social Green Flags:

· Maintains healthy friendships with good people
· Treats your friends and family with respect even if they're not particularly close
· Encourages your relationships with others
· Has some long-term friendships, indicating loyalty and relationship skills
· Is genuinely themselves around different people
· Shows interest in getting to know people who are important to you

Technology and Privacy Red Flags

Modern relationships involve navigating technology boundaries:
Technology Red Flags:

- Goes through your phone, email, or social media without permission
- Hides their phone or becomes secretive about their online activities
- Maintains active dating profiles while in a relationship with you
- Communicates inappropriately with ex-partners or potential romantic interests
- Posts or shares things about your relationship without your consent
- Uses technology to monitor, track, or control your activities

Technology Green Flags:

- Maintains appropriate privacy while being transparent about important matters
- Doesn't hide their phone but respects your privacy as well
- Has deleted dating apps and isn't seeking romantic attention from others
- Maintains appropriate boundaries with ex-partners and members of the opposite sex
- Asks before posting photos or information about you on social media
- Uses technology to enhance your relationship rather than create problems

Mental Health and Addiction Considerations

Mental health challenges aren't automatically red flags, but the way someone handles them can be:

Mental Health Red Flags:

- Refuses to acknowledge obvious mental health issues
- Won't seek professional help for problems that affect the relationship
- Uses mental health issues as an excuse for harmful behavior
- Expects you to be their therapist or sole source of support
- Becomes abusive or dangerous during mental health episodes
- Makes no effort to manage their mental health responsibly

Mental Health Green Flags:

- Acknowledges their mental health challenges honestly
- Seeks appropriate professional help when needed
- Takes responsibility for managing their mental health
- Has a support system beyond just you
- Doesn't use mental health issues to justify harmful behavior toward others
- Communicates about their needs without making you responsible for their emotional well-being

The Timing of Red Flags

Immediate deal breakers (first few dates):

- Any form of physical, verbal, or emotional abuse
- Lying about major life facts (marital status, children, employment)

- Illegal activity or serious substance abuse problems
- Disrespect toward you or service workers
- Pressuring you for sex or ignoring your boundaries

Watch carefully (early relationship):

- Inconsistent behavior or communication patterns
- Jealousy or possessiveness
- Financial irresponsibility or secrecy
- Bad relationships with family and friends
- Different values on important issues

Address directly (established relationship):

- Unwillingness to commit or discuss the future
- Not supporting your goals and dreams
- Consistent criticism or making you feel inadequate
- Refusal to work on relationship problems
- Ongoing conflicts about fundamental lifestyle differences

When Friends and Family Are Concerned

Sometimes people close to you can see red flags that you're missing:
Take seriously when multiple trusted people express concerns about:

- How your partner treats you
- Changes they've noticed in your behavior or happiness
- Concerning things they've witnessed or heard
- Their gut feelings about your partner's character

However, also consider:

- Whether their concerns are based on observation or assumption
- If they have their own motivations for disliking your partner
- Whether cultural or generational differences are influencing their judgment
- If their concerns are about genuine red flags or just personal preferences

Working Through Yellow Flags

Some behaviors fall into a gray area—they're concerning but not necessarily relationship-ending:

Yellow flags might include:

- Mild jealousy that can be addressed through communication
- Different communication styles that create misunderstandings
- Stress-related behavior changes that are temporary
- Minor financial disagreements that can be negotiated
- Family or social situations that are complex but not deal-breaking

Address yellow flags by:

- Having direct conversations about your concerns
- Setting clear boundaries and expectations
- Observing whether behavior changes after discussion
- Seeking couples therapy if needed
- Giving reasonable time for improvement while protecting your own well-being

Real-World Example: The Improvement vs. Excuse Cycle

When Liam started dating Becca, he noticed she had a tendency to be critical and dismissive during conversations. When he addressed this with her, Becca apologized and explained she was stressed about work. Over the following months, Liam observed the pattern:

- Becca would be critical or dismissive
- Liam would address it
- Becca would apologize and provide an excuse (work stress, family drama, being tired)
- The behavior would improve briefly, then return

"I realized that Becca wasn't actually changing her behavior—she was just getting better at apologizing and finding excuses," Liam explained. "She was managing my reactions to her behavior rather than changing the behavior itself."

Eventually, Liam recognized that this was a red flag pattern: acknowledgment without genuine change. He ended the relationship when it became clear that Becca wasn't willing to do the work to actually modify her behavior.

Building Your Green Flag Assessment Skills

- **Pay attention to patterns rather than isolated incidents**
- **Notice how someone treats people who can't do anything for them**
- **Observe behavior during stress, conflict, and disappointment**
- **Listen to how they talk about past relationships and other people**
- **Watch for consistency between words and actions over time**
- **Trust your gut feelings while also gathering factual information**

Self-Reflection: Your Own Flags

It's also important to assess your own behavior patterns:
Ask yourself:

- What red flags might you be displaying to potential partners?
- Do you have patterns of behavior that are concerning or unhealthy?
- Are you working on your own issues or expecting others to accept problematic behavior?
- What green flags do you consistently demonstrate in relationships?

Being the kind of partner who displays green flags increases your chances of attracting someone who also displays them.

Key Takeaways

- Red flags are warning signs that deserve attention; deal breakers should end relationships
- Green flags indicate healthy relationship potential and good character
- Focus on consistent patterns of behavior rather than potential or isolated incidents
- Pay attention to how someone treats others, manages stress, and handles conflict
- Technology, financial behavior, and social relationships all provide important information
- Trust input from friends and family, but also trust your own observations
- Work on displaying your own green flags while learning to recognize them in others

Action Steps

1. **Assess Your Current Relationship:** If you're in a relationship, honestly evaluate what red and green flags you're seeing. Are there patterns you've been ignoring?
2. **Trust Your Observations:** Make a list of specific behaviors you've noticed, not just your feelings about them. What patterns do you see?
3. **Seek Outside Perspective:** Talk to trusted friends or family about their observations of your relationship dynamics.
4. **Address Yellow Flags:** If there are concerning but not deal-breaking behaviors, have direct conversations about them and observe whether real change occurs.
5. **Work on Your Own Green Flags:** Identify ways you can be a healthier, more attractive partner yourself.
6. **Set Clear Boundaries:** Decide what behaviors you will and won't accept in a relationship, and stick to those boundaries.

The goal isn't to find a perfect person—everyone has flaws and areas for growth. The goal is to find someone whose character, values, and behavior patterns indicate they can be a healthy, supportive, growth-oriented partner.

The women in your life deserve to be treated with respect, kindness, and genuine care. But you also deserve to be in relationships with people who treat you well and contribute positively to your life.

Learning to recognize both red and green flags helps you make better relationship decisions and increases your chances of building the kind of partnership that enhances both people's lives rather than creating ongoing stress and conflict.

18

The Confident Man's Guide to Vulnerability

"I thought being strong meant never showing weakness. I didn't realize that hiding my real self was actually the weakest thing I could do."

This reflection from Marcus captures one of the biggest obstacles many men face in relationships: the belief that vulnerability equals weakness, and that showing your real emotions, fears, or struggles will make you less attractive or respectable.

But research consistently shows the opposite: appropriate vulnerability is one of the most attractive and relationship-building qualities a person can have. It's what allows real intimacy, trust, and connection to develop. The problem isn't vulnerability itself—it's understanding what healthy vulnerability looks like and how to practice it without overwhelming your partner or compromising your own emotional well-being.

Redefining Strength

Traditional definitions of masculinity often equate strength with emotional invulnerability—never showing fear, sadness, uncertainty, or need for support. But this definition creates men who are emotionally

251

isolated and partners who feel shut out from their inner world.
True strength includes:

- Being honest about your feelings without being controlled by them
- Asking for support when you need it while still taking responsibility for your life
- Admitting mistakes and learning from them rather than defending your ego
- Sharing your fears and insecurities with trusted people
- Being open about your struggles while working actively to address them
- Expressing love and affection without shame or embarrassment

False strength includes:

- Pretending you never have doubts, fears, or emotional needs
- Refusing help even when you're struggling unnecessarily
- Never admitting when you're wrong or don't know something
- Hiding all emotional experiences from your partner
- Acting like you don't care about things that actually matter deeply to you
- Equating emotional expression with weakness or failure

What Vulnerability Actually Is

Vulnerability isn't about emotional dumping or being needy. It's about authentic sharing of your inner experience when it's appropriate and relationship-building.
Healthy vulnerability includes:

- Sharing your genuine feelings about things that matter to you

- Admitting when you don't know something or need help
- Expressing appreciation and love openly
- Talking about your fears and insecurities when relevant
- Being honest about your mistakes and apologizing sincerely
- Sharing your dreams and hopes even when they feel risky

Unhealthy vulnerability includes:

- Using emotional sharing to manipulate or control others
- Overwhelming your partner with constant emotional processing
- Sharing intimate details inappropriately or too early in relationships
- Making your partner responsible for managing your emotional state
- Using vulnerability as an excuse for not taking responsibility for your actions
- Sharing without boundaries or consideration for the other person's capacity

Real-World Example: The Work Stress Transformation

When James lost a major client at his consulting firm, his first instinct was to handle the crisis alone. He became distant and stressed at home but told his wife Sarah only that work was "a bit busy."

Sarah could tell something was wrong but felt shut out when James insisted everything was fine. The distance between them grew as James became more stressed and Sarah became more confused about why he seemed upset with her.

The turning point came when James realized his attempt to "protect" Sarah was actually damaging their relationship. He sat down with her and shared what was really happening:

"I lost the Morrison account, and I'm worried about my job security. I've been afraid to tell you because I didn't want you to worry, but I realize I've been handling this stress badly and taking it out on you."

Sarah's response surprised James: "I knew something was wrong, and I was imagining all sorts of things. I'm much more worried when I don't know what's happening than when I know what we're actually dealing with."

Together, they made a plan for how to handle the potential financial impact, and Sarah offered emotional support that helped James navigate the crisis more effectively. James kept his job, but more importantly, he learned that sharing his struggles made him a better partner, not a weaker one.

The Timing of Vulnerability

Vulnerability requires good judgment about when, how much, and with whom to share:

Early relationship vulnerability might include:

- Sharing your genuine interests and passions
- Admitting when you don't know something or are nervous
- Expressing appreciation and positive feelings
- Being honest about your dating intentions
- Sharing appropriate stories about your life experiences

Established relationship vulnerability might include:

- Discussing fears about the future or your relationship
- Sharing childhood experiences that shaped you
- Expressing insecurities about work, appearance, or capabilities
- Talking about family dynamics and how they affect you

- Being honest about your emotional needs and struggles

Deep relationship vulnerability might include:

- Sharing your deepest fears and hopes
- Discussing past traumas and how they affect you
- Being honest about sexual desires and insecurities
- Expressing your most important values and beliefs
- Sharing your vision for your life and relationship

The Fear Behind the Mask

Many men avoid vulnerability because of specific fears:

Fear of being seen as weak: Worrying that showing emotion will make you seem less capable or masculine.

Fear of being rejected: Believing that your real self isn't loveable or acceptable.

Fear of being used against you: Worrying that sharing vulnerabilities will give others ammunition to hurt you.

Fear of being overwhelmed: Believing that if you start feeling emotions deeply, you won't be able to stop or control them.

Fear of being a burden: Worrying that sharing struggles will overwhelm or burden your partner.

Most of these fears are based on childhood experiences or cultural messages rather than reality. In healthy relationships, appropriate vulnerability actually increases attraction and connection rather than decreasing it.

Real-World Example: The Anxiety Admission

When Trevor started experiencing anxiety attacks during a stressful period at work, he was embarrassed and tried to hide them from his girlfriend Lauren. He made excuses to avoid social events, left gatherings early, and became increasingly withdrawn.

Lauren noticed the changes but couldn't understand what was happening. "Trevor seemed like he didn't want to spend time with me anymore," she explained later.

When Trevor finally admitted he was struggling with anxiety, Lauren's reaction was supportive and practical: "Why didn't you tell me sooner? My brother went through this same thing. There are things that can help."

Trevor was amazed by Lauren's response: "I thought she'd see me as broken or weak. Instead, she saw me as someone going through a difficult time who needed support. It actually brought us closer together."

Trevor got professional help for his anxiety and learned that sharing his struggle with Lauren had made him a better partner, not a more burdensome one.

Vulnerability in Different Areas

Emotional vulnerability: Sharing your feelings about situations, relationships, and life experiences.

Intellectual vulnerability: Admitting when you don't understand something or are uncertain about decisions.

Physical vulnerability: Being honest about health concerns, physical insecurities, or changes in your body.

Professional vulnerability: Sharing work struggles, career doubts, or professional insecurities.

Spiritual vulnerability: Discussing your beliefs, values, and questions about meaning and purpose.

Relational vulnerability: Being honest about your needs, fears, and experiences in the relationship itself.

The Gradual Approach

You don't need to share everything at once. Healthy vulnerability is often gradual:

Start with lower-risk sharing:

- Express genuine appreciation and positive feelings
- Admit when you don't know something or need help with practical matters
- Share excitement about things you're passionate about
- Be honest about minor mistakes or frustrations

Progress to medium-risk sharing:

- Discuss work stress or career concerns
- Share family dynamics that affect you
- Express insecurities about capabilities or appearance
- Talk about friendship or social struggles

Build to higher-risk sharing:

- Discuss deep fears about the future or your relationship
- Share childhood experiences that shaped you
- Express your most important values and beliefs
- Be honest about past mistakes or failures that still affect you

Creating Safety for Vulnerability

Vulnerability requires emotional safety, which you can help create:
Create safety by:

- Sharing your own vulnerabilities appropriately
- Responding supportively when your partner is vulnerable
- Not using shared vulnerabilities against each other during arguments
- Respecting confidences and not sharing private information with others
- Avoiding judgment or criticism when someone shares something personal

Safety is damaged by:

- Mocking or minimizing someone's vulnerable sharing
- Using personal information as ammunition during conflicts
- Sharing private details with friends or family without permission
- Responding to vulnerability with advice-giving instead of support
- Making someone feel like their emotions are inconvenient or problematic

Vulnerability vs. Emotional Dumping

Healthy vulnerability:

- Considers the other person's capacity and timing
- Includes your own responsibility and efforts to address problems
- Invites connection and support rather than demanding solutions
- Is appropriate to the relationship level and context

- Includes emotional regulation and self-awareness

Emotional dumping:

- Overwhelms the other person without consideration for their capacity
- Makes the other person responsible for fixing your emotional state
- Happens without boundaries or awareness of appropriateness
- Is used to avoid taking responsibility for your own emotional work
- Lacks self-awareness about impact on others

Real-World Example: The Father Relationship Revelation

When Paul's father was diagnosed with Alzheimer's, he initially tried to handle all the practical and emotional challenges alone. His partner Jennifer could see he was stressed but felt helpless when he insisted he was handling everything fine.

The breakthrough came when Paul realized he was recreating the same emotional distance his father had always maintained. In a moment of honest reflection, he shared with Jennifer:

"I'm scared about losing my dad, but I'm even more scared about becoming like him. He never let anyone help him or showed any vulnerability, and now I realize I'm doing the same thing. I don't want to push you away like he pushed all of us away."

This vulnerable admission opened the door for Jennifer to provide real support, and for Paul to process his complex feelings about his father's illness and their relationship. "Admitting I was scared and needed help didn't make me weak," Paul realized later. "It made me more like the kind of man I actually wanted to be."

Vulnerability in Conflict

Being vulnerable during disagreements can transform conflicts from battles into opportunities for deeper understanding:
Vulnerable conflict communication includes:

- "I felt hurt when..." instead of "You always..."
- "I'm scared that..." instead of accusations about motives
- "I need..." instead of criticism about what they're doing wrong
- "I'm sorry I..." instead of defensive explanations
- "Help me understand..." instead of attacking their position

This doesn't mean avoiding difficult conversations or not standing up for yourself. It means engaging with difficult topics from a place of authenticity rather than defensiveness.

Building Vulnerability Skills

Practice self-awareness: Regularly check in with your own emotions and needs rather than just focusing on external circumstances.

Start small: Begin with low-risk vulnerability and build gradually as you develop comfort and skill.

Choose your audience: Share appropriately vulnerable information with people who have earned your trust and shown they can handle it well.

Balance sharing and listening: Vulnerability should be reciprocal rather than one-sided dumping.

Work on emotional regulation: Develop skills for managing your emotions so you can share them without being overwhelmed by them.

Learn from feedback: Pay attention to how others respond to your vulnerability and adjust your approach accordingly.

The Professional Context

Workplace vulnerability looks different from personal relationship vulnerability but can still be valuable:
Professional vulnerability might include:

- Admitting when you don't understand something and need clarification
- Asking for help or mentoring when facing new challenges
- Sharing appropriate concerns about project timelines or resources
- Expressing genuine enthusiasm for work that excites you
- Acknowledging mistakes and focusing on solutions

Professional boundaries include:

- Not sharing personal relationship or family problems with colleagues
- Avoiding emotional dumping about work stress on coworkers
- Not using vulnerability to avoid accountability for performance issues

The Long-Term Benefits

Men who learn to be appropriately vulnerable in relationships experience:

Deeper intimacy: Partners feel closer to someone they really know rather than someone wearing a mask.

Better support: People can only help you with struggles they know about.

Reduced isolation: Sharing your inner world connects you to others rather than leaving you alone with your experiences.

Authentic relationships: Connections based on who you really are rather than who you think you should be.

Personal growth: Honest self-reflection and sharing promotes continued development.

Better conflict resolution: Vulnerable communication resolves issues more effectively than defensive fighting.

Common Vulnerability Mistakes

The overshare: Sharing too much too quickly, overwhelming the other person.

The performance: Using vulnerability as a technique to get specific responses rather than authentic sharing.

The dump and run: Sharing something important then immediately changing the subject or leaving.

The neediness trap: Using vulnerability to make others responsible for your emotional state.

The timing disaster: Choosing inappropriate moments for serious emotional sharing.

The audience error: Sharing intimate details with people who haven't earned that level of trust.

Vulnerability with Male Friends

Men often struggle with vulnerability in friendships as well as romantic relationships:

Healthy male friendship vulnerability might include:

· Asking friends for advice during difficult times
· Sharing genuine excitement about personal achievements
· Admitting when you're struggling with work, relationships, or life

decisions
· Expressing appreciation for the friendship itself
· Being honest about fears and insecurities when relevant

This doesn't mean turning every social interaction into a therapy session, but it does mean allowing real connection beyond just surface-level activities.

Cultural and Family Considerations

Your comfort with vulnerability may be influenced by:

Cultural background: Some cultures encourage emotional expression while others discourage it.

Family patterns: How emotions were handled in your family of origin affects your comfort with vulnerability.

Peer influences: The men around you may model more or less emotional openness.

Professional environment: Some work cultures are more or less accepting of emotional expression.

Understanding these influences helps you make conscious choices about vulnerability rather than just following inherited patterns.

Advanced Vulnerability Skills

Reading the room: Understanding when others are capable of receiving vulnerable sharing vs. when they need different kinds of interaction.

Reciprocal vulnerability: Gauging appropriate levels of sharing based on what others are comfortable sharing with you.

Boundary setting: Knowing what you're comfortable sharing and what you prefer to keep private.

Support seeking: Asking for the kind of support you actually need rather than hoping others will guess.

Emotional regulation: Managing your emotions while sharing them rather than being overwhelmed by feelings.

Key Takeaways

- True strength includes the ability to be vulnerable appropriately, not emotional invulnerability
- Healthy vulnerability builds intimacy and connection rather than creating burden or weakness
- Timing, audience, and boundaries are crucial for effective vulnerable sharing
- Vulnerability requires emotional safety, which you can help create in your relationships
- The fear of vulnerability is often based on old messages rather than current reality
- Gradual vulnerability allows you to build comfort and skills over time
- Vulnerability in conflict transforms battles into opportunities for understanding

Action Steps

1. **Assess Your Vulnerability Comfort Level:** Reflect on how comfortable you are sharing different types of personal information. What fears hold you back from being more open?
2. **Practice Low-Risk Vulnerability:** This week, share something genuine but not too risky with someone you trust—perhaps expressing appreciation or admitting you don't know something.
3. **Identify Your Support Network:** List the people in your life who you could share different types of struggles or concerns with. Do

you have adequate support?

4. **Work on Emotional Awareness:** Spend time each day checking in with your own emotions and needs rather than just focusing on external tasks.

5. **Share One Real Thing:** Have one conversation this week where you share something authentic about your current experience—a stress, hope, fear, or excitement.

6. **Practice Vulnerable Conflict:** Next time you have a disagreement with someone important, try leading with vulnerability ("I felt hurt when...") instead of defensiveness.

The women in your life don't want to be with someone who pretends to be invulnerable. They want to be with someone real—someone who has struggles and fears and dreams, someone who can admit when they need support, someone who trusts them enough to share their authentic self.

That kind of vulnerability isn't weakness—it's one of the most courageous and attractive qualities a person can have. And it's the foundation of every meaningful relationship you'll ever build.

Conclusion

It's Actually Pretty Simple

"The best relationship advice I ever got was: treat her like a human being you genuinely care about, and everything else will follow."

This wisdom from my friend David, married happily for fifteen years, captures what I hope you've learned from this book: understanding women isn't actually that complicated. The complexity comes from all the myths, games, and artificial strategies we've been taught to believe are necessary.

At its core, building great relationships with women is about the same thing as building great relationships with anyone: seeing them as complete, complex individuals deserving of respect, care, and genuine interest. The difference is that many men have never been taught how to do this effectively.

What You've Learned

Over these eighteen chapters, we've covered a lot of ground. But if I had to summarize the key insights, they would be these:

Authenticity beats strategy every time. The pickup lines, games, and manipulation tactics don't work because they're trying to trick someone into liking a person who doesn't actually exist. When you show up as your genuine self—with your real interests, values, and

266

personality—you attract people who actually like you for who you are. **Emotional intelligence is learnable and essential.** Most men weren't taught to recognize, understand, or respond to emotional communication. But these skills can be developed, and they dramatically improve every relationship in your life.

Self-sufficiency is attractive. Women want partners, not projects. When you can manage your own life, emotions, and responsibilities, you become someone who enhances their life rather than someone who needs to be managed.

Communication is the foundation of everything. Real listening, honest sharing, and the ability to navigate conflict constructively are more important than compatibility, physical attraction, or shared interests.

Respect means seeing her as an equal. Not someone to protect, improve, or manage, but someone whose thoughts, feelings, and decisions deserve the same consideration you'd want for yourself.

Daily actions matter more than grand gestures. Relationships are built through thousands of small interactions that either create connection or distance. Consistency beats intensity every time.

Growth and vulnerability strengthen relationships. The strongest partnerships are between two people who are committed to becoming better versions of themselves and who can share their authentic experiences, including struggles and fears.

The Paradox of Simplicity

Here's something interesting: the more you understand about relationships, the simpler they become. When you're focused on games and strategies, every interaction feels complicated. When you're focused on genuine care and connection, most relationship "problems" resolve themselves naturally.

Women aren't mysterious creatures who require special codes to understand. They're individuals with their own thoughts, feelings, experiences, and preferences. The "mystery" disappears when you approach them with genuine curiosity rather than assumptions about what all women want.

The "complexity" of female communication becomes clear when you develop basic emotional intelligence and listening skills. The "difficulty" of maintaining long-term relationships becomes manageable when you understand that love is both a feeling and a practice.

What This Isn't

This book isn't a magic formula that will guarantee romantic success with every woman you meet. It's not a manipulation manual designed to help you "get" women through psychological tricks. And it's definitely not a promise that following these principles will eliminate all relationship challenges.

What this book is: a guide to becoming the kind of person who can build genuine, satisfying, lasting relationships based on mutual respect, understanding, and care.

Some women won't be interested in you, and that's perfectly fine. Some relationships won't work out despite your best efforts, and that's normal too. The goal isn't to be irresistible to everyone—it's to be genuinely attractive to people who are compatible with the real you.

The Ripple Effects

Here's something most relationship books don't tell you: when you develop these skills, they improve every area of your life, not just your romantic relationships.

Better communication skills make you more effective at work, a better friend, and a more engaged family member.

Emotional intelligence helps you navigate workplace conflicts, understand client needs, and lead teams more effectively.

Self-sufficiency and emotional regulation reduce your stress and increase your overall life satisfaction.

The ability to support others' growth makes you a mentor, leader, and friend that people value and trust.

Conflict resolution skills help you handle disagreements in every context, from family disputes to professional negotiations.

You're not just becoming a better partner—you're becoming a better person.

The Cultural Shift

I hope this book contributes to a larger cultural shift in how we think about masculinity and relationships. The old model—where men were supposed to be emotionally invulnerable providers and women were supposed to be dependent caretakers—doesn't work for most people in the modern world.

The new model is partnership between equals: two people who can both provide and receive care, who can both be strong and vulnerable, who can both pursue their individual goals and support each other's growth.

This isn't about men becoming more like women or abandoning masculine qualities. It's about expanding our definition of what it means to be a strong, attractive, successful man to include emotional intelligence, genuine care for others, and the ability to form deep, authentic connections.

The Long View

Building great relationships is a long-term project, not a quick fix. The men who are most successful in love are those who commit to ongoing growth and development rather than looking for shortcuts or silver bullets.

This means:

· Continuing to work on your communication skills throughout your life
· Staying curious about the people you care about as they grow and change
· Being willing to adapt your approach as you learn more about yourself and relationships
· Treating each relationship as an opportunity to become a better partner
· Understanding that mastery comes through practice, not just knowledge

Starting Where You Are

You don't have to be perfect to start implementing these principles. You don't need to overhaul your entire personality or wait until you've resolved all your personal issues.

Start where you are, with the relationships you have right now:

If you're single: Focus on becoming the kind of person you'd want to date. Work on your emotional intelligence, communication skills, and self-sufficiency. Practice these principles in your friendships and family relationships.

If you're dating: Be more authentic in your interactions. Listen better. Ask more meaningful questions. Support the goals and dreams of people you care about.

If you're in a long-term relationship: Begin daily practices of appreciation and connection. Have deeper conversations. Work on yourself while supporting your partner's growth.

If you're struggling with relationship problems: Focus on what you can control—your own behavior, communication, and approach to the relationship. Seek professional help if needed.

The Courage to Be Real

Perhaps the biggest theme of this book is the courage to be real—to show up as your authentic self rather than performing a character you think women want to see.

This can feel scary. What if your real self isn't good enough? What if people don't like the person you actually are when you stop trying to impress them?

But here's the truth: your authentic self is the only self that can build genuinely satisfying relationships. And the person you really are— with your unique combination of strengths, interests, values, and yes, even flaws—is worthy of love and connection.

The women who are right for you will appreciate your authenticity, not be turned off by it. The ones who aren't interested in the real you weren't right for you anyway.

A Personal Note

Writing this book has been a journey of reflection on my own relation- ship experiences and mistakes. I haven't always practiced what I'm preaching here. I've been the guy who tried to use strategies instead of authenticity, who avoided vulnerability, who didn't listen well enough, and who took partners for granted.

The principles in this book aren't theoretical—they're learned through real experience, including the pain of relationships that could have been better if I'd understood these concepts earlier.

If you recognize yourself in some of the negative examples in this book, don't despair. Growth is possible at any age and any stage of life. The men who become great partners aren't the ones who never made mistakes—they're the ones who learned from their mistakes and committed to doing better.

The Women in Your Life

As you implement these principles, remember that every woman you encounter—whether romantically, professionally, or socially—is someone's daughter, sister, mother, or friend. She has her own dreams, fears, struggles, and achievements. She has her own story that's just as complex and important as yours.

When you approach women with this awareness, it naturally leads to the respect, curiosity, and genuine care that form the foundation of all good relationships.

The women in your life don't need you to be perfect. They need you to be real, present, supportive, and committed to growth. They need you to see them as complete individuals rather than puzzles to solve or prizes to win.

Moving Forward

You now have the knowledge. The question is: what will you do with it?

Knowledge without action is just entertainment. These principles only work if you practice them consistently, not just when you remember or when it's convenient.

Start small. Pick one or two concepts from this book and focus on implementing them in your daily life. Practice better listening in one conversation this week. Express genuine appreciation to someone you care about. Work on being more emotionally available when someone shares something important with you.

As these practices become natural, add more. Build your skills gradually but consistently. Remember that becoming a great partner is a lifelong journey, not a destination you arrive at and then stop working on.

The Ultimate Truth

Here's what I hope you remember from this book: understanding women isn't about cracking a code or learning secret techniques. It's about becoming a genuinely good person who can form authentic connections with other human beings.

When you focus on being someone worth knowing—someone who listens well, communicates honestly, supports others' growth, and shows up authentically in relationships—you naturally become attractive to people who share your values and appreciate your genuine self.

The best relationships aren't built on perfect compatibility or flawless execution of romantic strategies. They're built on two people who genuinely like and respect each other, who support each other's growth, and who choose to keep working on their connection even when it's challenging.

You have everything you need to build relationships like this. You always did. You just needed to understand how to access and develop these natural human capacities for connection, empathy, and love.

The women in your life are waiting for partners who can see them clearly, appreciate them genuinely, and love them authentically. They're waiting for men who understand that the best relationships are partnerships between equals, not games to be won or puzzles to be solved.

That man can be you. In fact, he already is you—you just needed permission to let him out.

The game-playing, strategy-using, emotionally-unavailable version of masculinity is outdated and ineffective. The future belongs to men who can combine strength with vulnerability, independence with partnership, and confidence with genuine care for others.

Welcome to the future. The women in your life are going to love meeting the real you.

Final Thought

Love isn't complicated. People are complex, relationships require skill and effort, and modern life creates challenges our grandparents never faced. But love itself—the genuine care, appreciation, and commitment that builds lasting partnerships—is simple.

See her. Hear her. Respect her. Support her growth. Share your authentic self. Work on your own development. Handle conflict with maturity. Show up consistently with care and attention.

It really is that simple. And it really is that transformative.

Now go build some beautiful relationships.

Printed in Dunstable, United Kingdom